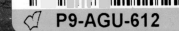

P9-AGU-612

WRANGELL-SAINT ELIAS

International Mountain Wilderness

Alaska Geographic®
Volume 8, Number 1, 1981

The Alaska Geographic Society

To teach many more to better know and use our natural resources

About This Issue: Gerald Wright, National Park Service specialist in the Wrangell Mountains, built the foundation for this issue. Gil Mull generously contributed his knowledge of the region's physical environment and mountaineering history. George Herben, who first visited Kennecott in the early 1950s, added his knowledge of the history of the Wrangells and contributed many of the magnificent photos. The wardens and naturalists at Kluane National Park, particularly Jack Schick, were especially helpful in pulling together information for the Saint Elias area in Canada.

We thank the many photographers whose fine photos helped to convey to readers the grandeur of the Wrangell-Saint Elias wilderness. And we are grateful for the help of reviewers, especially Katherine Ashby and Nancy Gross, for their insightful comments.

Editors: Robert A. Henning, Barbara Olds, Penny Rennick
Editorial Assistance: Jerrianne Lowther
Designer: Dianne Hofbeck
Cartographer: Jon.Hersh

Copyright©1981 by
The Alaska Geographic Society
All rights reserved.
Registered trademark: **Alaska Geographic**
ISSN 0361-1353; Key title **Alaska Geographic**

Library of Congress cataloging in publication data:
Wright, Gerald, 1943-
    Wrangell-Saint Elias.

    (Alaska geographic; v. 8, no. 1 ISSN 0361-1353)
    1. Wrangell Mountains, Alaska.   2. Saint Elias
Mountains.   I. Mull, Gil, joint author.   II. Herben,
George, joint author.   III. Title.   IV. Series.
F901.A266   vol. 8, no. 1   [F912.W72]   917.98s
ISBN 0-88240-149-1   [979.8'3]   80-26210

STATEMENT OF OWNERSHIP MANAGEMENT and CIRCULATION

(Required by 39 U.S.C. 3685)

Alaska Geographic® is a quarterly publication, home offices, Box 4-EEE, Anchorage, Alaska 99509. Editor is Robert A. Henning. Publisher is The Alaska Geographic Society, Box 4-EEE, Anchorage, Alaska 99509. Owners are Robert A. Henning and Phyllis G. Henning, Box 4-EEE, Anchorage, Alaska 99509. Robert A. Henning and Phyllis Henning, husband and wife, are owners of 100 percent of all common stock outstanding.

Alaska Geographic® has a paid circulation of 15,048 subscribers and newsstand buyers.

I certify that statements above are correct and complete:

ROBERT A. HENNING
Editor

ALASKA GEOGRAPHIC®, ISSN 0361-1353, is published quarterly by The Alaska Geographic Society, Anchorage, Alaska 99509. Second-class postage paid in Edmonds, Washington 98020. Printed in U.S.A.

THE ALASKA GEOGRAPHIC SOCIETY is a non-profit organization exploring new frontiers of knowledge across the lands of the polar rim, learning how other men and other countries live in their Norths, putting the geography book back in the classroom, exploring new methods of teaching and learning—sharing in the excitement of discovery in man's wonderful new world north of 51°16'.

MEMBERS OF THE SOCIETY RECEIVE *Alaska Geographic®*, a quality magazine in color which devotes each quarterly issue to monographic in-depth coverage of a northern geographic region or resource-oriented subject.

MEMBERSHIP DUES in The Alaska Geographic Society are $20 per year; $24 to non-U.S. addresses. (Eighty percent of each year's dues is for a one-year subscription to *Alaska Geographic®*.) Order from The Alaska Geographic Society, Box 4-EEE, Anchorage, Alaska 99509; (907) 274-0521.

MATERIAL SOUGHT: The editors of *Alaska Geographic®* seek a wide variety of informative material on the lands north of 51°16' on geographic subjects—anything to do with resources and their uses (with heavy emphasis on quality color photography)—from Alaska, Northern Canada, Siberia, Japan—all geographic areas that have a relationship to Alaska in a physical or economic sense. In early 1981 editors were seeking material on the following geographic regions and subjects: Alaska fish and fisheries, the Seward Peninsula, and Canada's Northwest Territories. We do not want material done in excessive scientific terminology. A query to the editors is suggested. Payments are made for all material upon publication.

CHANGE OF ADDRESS: The post office does not automatically forward *Alaska Geographic®* when you move. To insure continuous service, notify us six weeks before moving. Send us your new address and zip code (and moving date), your old address and zip code, and if possible send a mailing label from a copy of *Alaska Geographic®*. Send this information to *Alaska Geographic®* Mailing Offices, 130 Second Avenue South, Edmonds, Washington 98020.

MAILING LISTS: We have begun making our members' names and addresses available to carefully screened publications and companies whose products and activities might be of interest to you. If you would prefer not to receive such mailings, please so advise us, and include your mailing label (or your name and address if label is not available).

The Cover • *Massive Mount Logan (19,850 feet) and pointed Mount Augusta (14,070 feet) dominate the skyline in this view of the Saint Elias Mountains.*
• GEORGE HERBEN

Contents page • *A climber approaches the summit of 19,850-foot Mount Logan, highest peak in Canada and second highest in North America.*
• THOMAS McCULLOUGH

Left • *Regal (left) and Rohn glaciers join northeast of McCarthy and flow to Nizina Glacier. Regal Mountain (13,845 feet) rises in the distance.*
• GEORGE HERBEN

Overleaf • *One lobe of Lowell Glacier terminates at the Alsek River in southern Kluane National Park.*
• W. B. LIDDLE, COURTESY OF PARKS CANADA

3

Introduction

Editors' note: As this issue of *ALASKA GEOGRAPHIC®* went to press, President Jimmy Carter signed a bill establishing the Wrangell-Saint Elias National Park and Preserve. We have made every effort to include the most current information but government agencies had not worked out specifics on management of this area at press time.

The Wrangell and Saint Elias mountain ranges occupy a 20-million-acre region stretching eastward from the Copper River in southcentral Alaska through western Yukon Territory and northwestern British Columbia. These lands constitute one of North America's outstanding mountain wilderness resources.

Passage of the Alaska Native Claims Settlement Act (ANCSA) in 1971 authorized the Federal Government to withdraw and study federal lands in Alaska for their suitability for future uses. In December 1978, because of the region's scientific and cultural significance, President Carter, acting under authority of the 1908 Antiquities Act, designated 10,950,000 acres within Alaska as Wrangell-Saint Elias National Monument, leaving open the option for Congress to consider national park status. In December 1980 President Jimmy Carter signed a bill creating the Wrangell-Saint Elias National Park and Preserve. In the Yukon, most land within the Saint Elias Mountains falls within 5,400,000-acre Kluane National Park, set aside in 1972 and officially proclaimed in 1976 out of lands constituting the larger Kluane Game Sanctuary established in 1943.

For the most part the Wrangell and Saint Elias ranges share a common geologic, ecologic, and cultural heritage. They form a distinct landscape unit, separated on the west and northwest from adjacent areas by the Copper River. The Tetlin lowlands extending into Yukon Territory, and the Gulf of Alaska form natural divides to the north and south respectively. The region's eastern boundary generally coincides with the eastern boundary of Kluane National Park and stretches southward to the Alsek River where it curves westward and follows the Alsek to the sea. Some visionaries foresee creation of an international park out of lands on both sides of the U.S.-Canada border which follows 141° longitude. This concept was advanced through recent joint United States and Canadian nomination and subsequent approval by the United Nations of lands in Wrangell-Saint Elias National Park and Preserve and Kluane National Park as a World Heritage Area. ••

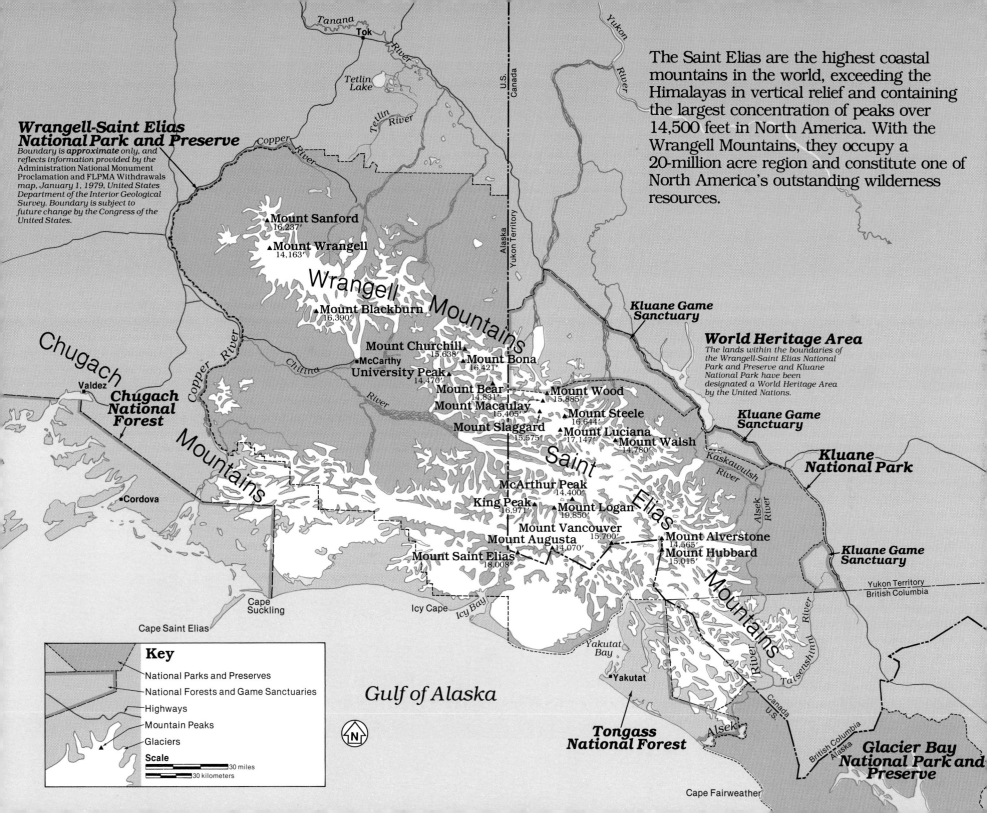

Tanana River

Tok

Tetlin Lake

Tetlin River

Copper River

U.S. / Canada

Yukon River

Alaska / Yukon Territory

Wrangell-Saint Elias National Park and Preserve
Boundary is **approximate** only, and reflects information provided by the Administration National Monument Proclamation and FLPMA Withdrawals map, January 1, 1979, United States Department of the Interior Geological Survey. Boundary is subject to future change by the Congress of the United States.

The Saint Elias are the highest coastal mountains in the world, exceeding the Himalayas in vertical relief and containing the largest concentration of peaks over 14,500 feet in North America. With the Wrangell Mountains, they occupy a 20-million acre region and constitute one of North America's outstanding wilderness resources.

▲ **Mount Sanford**
16,237′

▲ **Mount Wrangell**
14,163′

Wrangell Mountains

▲ Mount Blackburn
16,390′

Kluane Game Sanctuary

World Heritage Area
The lands within the boundaries of the Wrangell-Saint Elias National Park and Preserve and Kluane National Park have been designated a World Heritage Area by the United Nations.

Mount Churchill ▲
15,638′
■ McCarthy   ▲ **Mount Bona**
16,421′
University Peak
14,470′

Chugach Mountains

■ Valdez

Chugach National Forest

Chitina River

Copper River

Mount Bear ▲
14,831′   ▲ **Mount Wood**
Mount Macaulay ▲   15,885′
15,405′ ▲

▲ **Mount Steele**
16,644′

Kluane Game Sanctuary

Mount Slaggard ▲
15,575′   ▲ **Mount Luciana**
17,147′   ▲ **Mount Walsh**
14,780′

Saint

Kaskawulsh River

Kluane National Park

■ Cordova

McArthur Peak ▲
14,400′
King Peak ▲
16,971′   ▲ **Mount Logan**
19,850′

Elias

Alsek River

Mount Vancouver
15,700′   **Mount Alverstone**
14,565′
Mount Augusta   ▲ **Mount Hubbard**
14,070′   15,015′

Kluane Game Sanctuary

Mount Saint Elias ▲
18,008′

Mountains

Cape Suckling

Cape Saint Elias

Icy Cape   Icy Bay

Yakutat Bay

Tatshenshini River

Yukon Territory / British Columbia

Key
— National Parks and Preserves
— National Forests and Game Sanctuaries
— Highways
▲ Mountain Peaks
Glaciers

Scale
30 miles
30 kilometers

Gulf of Alaska

Ⓝ

■ Yakutat

Alsek River

Canada / U.S.

Tongass National Forest

British Columbia / Alaska

Glacier Bay National Park and Preserve

Cape Fairweather

The Lay of the Land

McArthur Peak rises above this panoramic view of the head of Logan Glacier in the Saint Elias Mountains. The glacier extends 50 miles from near Mount Logan in Canada to Chitina Glacier in Alaska.
• STEVE McCUTCHEON

The Wrangell, Saint Elias and Chugach

ranges create an international mountain wilderness. The ranges are part of the western North America cordillera and contain a wide diversity of rock types that exert a profound influence on topography. In geologic time, these mountains are very young; most recent uplifts of present ranges have occurred in the past 10 million years.

The Wrangell Mountains form a crescent north of the Chitina River basin and consist primarily of young, nearly horizontal lava flows resting on an older base of sediments, altered volcanics, and some granitic igneous rocks. Upon this foundation rise the major peaks in the range: Mount Bona (16,421 feet), Mount Blackburn (16,390 feet), Mount Sanford (16,237 feet), and Mount Drum (12,010 feet). All extinct volcanoes, these peaks are in various stages of erosion by glacial activity. The range's only active volcano, Mount Wrangell (14,163 feet), has been studied intensively for the past 20 years by Dr. Carl Benson of the University of Alaska. Since the 1964 Alaska earthquake, Mount Wrangell has undergone dramatic increases in heat flux and solfatara (volcanic vents which emit sulfurous gases or steam) activity. This has melted more than 500 million cubic yards of glacier ice from a single crater on the summit caldera's rim, and has affected some of the glaciers which radiate from the mountain.

Near the edge of the Copper River basin, just west of Mount Drum, three warm water mineral springs have built low cones of silt and clay that rise above the forest. These springs discharge variable amounts of carbon dioxide and nitrogen gas with the warm water, and have been called mud volcanoes. They are thought to be related to nearby volcanic activity and may indicate significant geothermal potential.

South of the Wrangells, the Chugach and Saint Elias mountains constitute a geologically distinct terrain primarily composed of metamorphosed and highly altered sedimentary and volcanic rocks intruded by a few granitic bodies. This range forms a broad east-west trending band separating the Chitina valley lowlands from the Gulf of Alaska. Where dissected by the Copper River, the chain is known as the Chugach Mountains. They have been extensively glaciated and average 7,000 to 8,000 feet in elevation, although three peaks — Mount Steller, Mount

Opposite •
Large mud volcanoes fume and boil near the western flanks of Mount Drum.
• RANSOM SALTMARCH

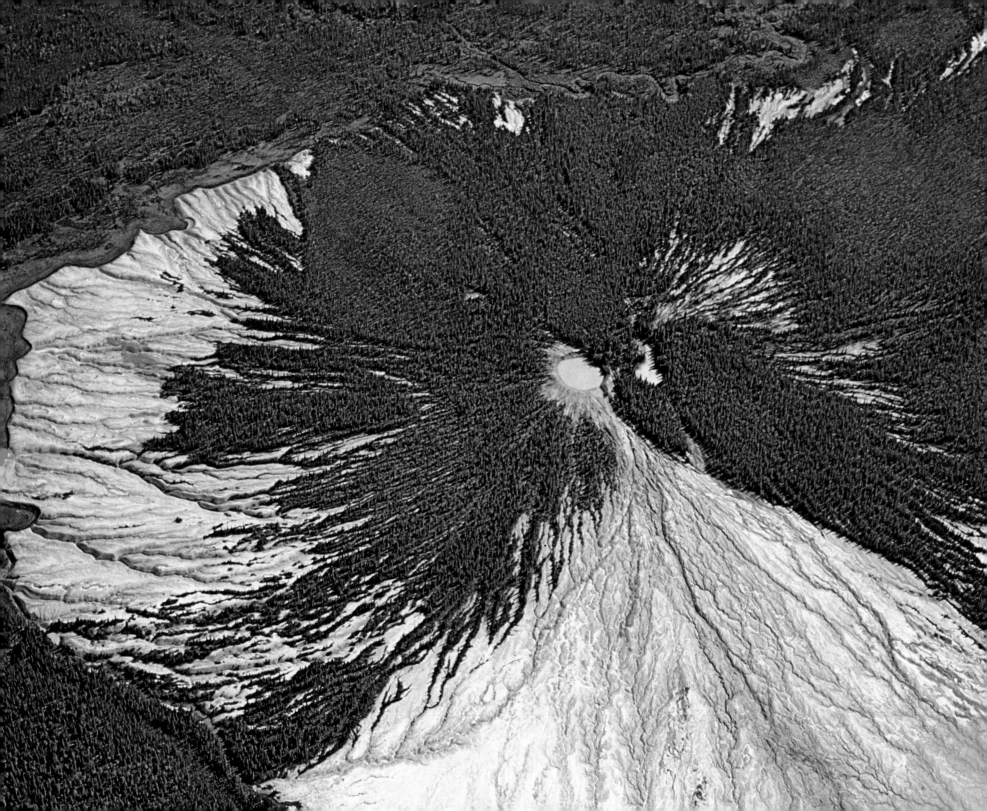

Clockwise from below

• *Lava from volcanic activity in the Wrangells has vented itself in many locations far removed from volcanic summits. On this ridge above the Chetaslina River, the remains of one of these upwellings forms a giant fang of rock.*
• RANSOM SALTMARCH

• *Lava cliffs in the Wrangells, lit by oblique rays of the late afternoon sun, appear slashed and bleeding. Iron-stained, erosional products frequently form at the interface between lava flows, then slide downslope to create these vivid swathes.*
• RANSOM SALTMARCH

• *Examples of columnar jointing are frequent in lava in the Wrangells. Fracture planes that divide the rock into these pillar-like segments form during cooling.*
• RANSOM SALTMARCH

• *Molten lava releases trapped gas as it cools, forming pits in the rock.*
• RANSOM SALTMARCH

• *Rock glaciers cover slopes in the Wrangells. These slides of broken rock mixed with ice, flow slowly down a slope much as glaciers do.*
• C. M. MOLENAAR

Right • *Mount Wrangell (14,163 feet) and Cheshnina Gorge. The dome rises nearly two miles above surrounding spurs, and tongues of ice flow five miles down its flanks.*
• RANSOM SALTMARCH

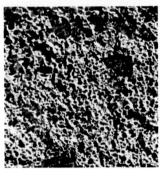

Mount Tom White (10,630 feet) and Martin River Glacier are dominant features of the Chugach Mountains. The glacier extends 25 miles from the head of Martin River to 20 miles northeast of Katalla.
• GIL MULL

Tom White, and Mount Hawkins — rise to more than 10,000 feet. East of the Copper River, large areas of the range are covered by interconnected ice fields, the most significant being Bagley Icefield which flows out through Bering Glacier.

To the east, the Chugach Mountains grade into the Saint Elias Mountains, also composed of altered sedimentary and volcanic rocks. The Saint Elias Mountains extend southeastward from the Chugach and Wrangell mountains across southwestern Yukon Territory and into northwestern British Columbia. Higher than the other ranges, these mountains have been more intensely glaciated and have many angular, multi-faceted peaks. The Saint Eliases are the highest coastal mountains in the world, and exceed the Himalayas in vertical relief.

The Saint Elias range contains the largest concentration of mountain peaks exceeding 14,500 feet in North America. Within 30 miles of the Gulf of Alaska, Mount Saint Elias, fourth highest on the continent, rises to 18,008 feet. Mount Vancouver pushes upward 15,700 feet, and Mount Hubbard rises to 15,015 feet. At the center of the range towers Mount Logan, at 19,850 feet — Canada's highest peak and the second highest in North America. Surrounding these and other peaks is a vast network of ice fields which feeds valley and piedmont glacial systems. Several glaciers flowing from the Saint Elias Mountains reach tidewater on the Gulf of Alaska.

Left • *Scientists traveling by helicopter had this view of Mount Saint Elias (18,008 feet) and Seward Glacier crevasse field from 5,000-foot Point Glorious, 49 miles northwest of Yakutat.*
• GIL MULL

Overleaf • *Mount Hubbard (15,015 feet) rises from Cathedral Glacier in the Saint Elias Mountains in Canada. Early mountaineer I. C. Russell named the peak for Gardiner G. Hubbard, founder and first president of the National Geographic Society.*
• CHLAUS LOTSCHER

15

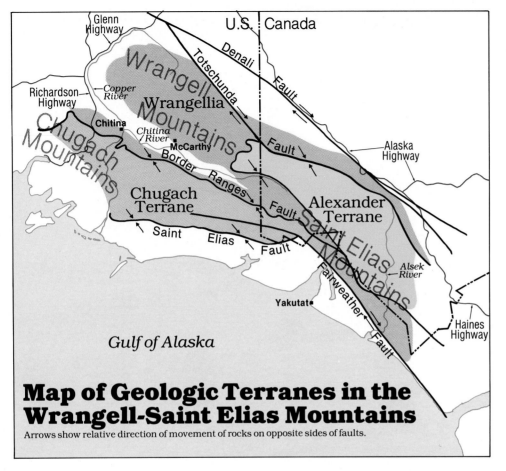

Map of Geologic Terranes in the Wrangell-Saint Elias Mountains

Arrows show relative direction of movement of rocks on opposite sides of faults.

The Wrangell Mountains contrast sharply in appearance with the adjacent Chugach and Saint Elias ranges. To a large extent this different appearance is caused by their radically different geological history. Volcanic rocks of the Wrangells in many places overlie a distinctive light gray, cliff-forming limestone unit known as Chitistone Limestone. This, in turn, overlies a thick, dark gray, altered volcanic formation known as Nikolai Greenstone.

Recent U.S. Geological Survey studies suggest that this part of Alaska, with its distinctive suite of rock units, was formerly at a much lower latitude and migrated into its present position from an area probably within 15° of the equator. This distinctive assemblage of rock types is known as Wrangellia. As it migrated to its present position, Wrangellia collided with another distinctive terrane composed of much older, highly contorted rocks that generally weather dark gray with numerous areas of light-gray-to-white, contorted marble. This terrane is known as the Alexander Terrane, and is found in Alaska near Barnard Glacier and Mount Bear north of the eastern end of the Chitina valley. The Alexander Terrane extends eastward into adjacent Yukon Territory.

To the south, a large portion of the Chugach and Saint Elias mountains constitute another distinctive suite of rocks known as the Chugach Terrane, which consists of complexly deformed deep sea sediments and associated altered volcanic rocks. These rocks probably formed an offshore island arc system that also migrated to its present position to collide with rocks of Wrangellia. The zone of collision is known as the Border Ranges fault, and extends along the southern side of the Chitina valley and eastward into the Yukon. Still another fault zone is found along the south side of the mountains. This zone, known as the Saint Elias fault, separates the altered rocks of the high mountain areas from the almost unaltered sedimentary rocks that underlie the coastal plain.

Geological and geophysical data suggest that migration of such large pieces of the earth's crust is driven by slow convection in the fluid or plastic interior of the earth; the rigid pieces of crust are thought to float on this material much as cakes of ice float on large

Black lava, reed lava, and amber chunks of consolidated ash color the Wrangell landscape. Frequently, high rivulets branch together as they wash down from their respective outcrops and the multicolored fragments come to rest in valley bottoms.
• RANSOM SALTMARCH

water bodies. Collisions of fragments of crust sometimes have a snowplowlike effect in which portions of crust are uplifted to form high mountains. Abundant evidence suggests that such a process is occurring at the present time to form the high Saint Elias Mountains, which in places contain relatively young rocks at high elevations. The highest parts of the Saint Elias and Wrangell mountains are in areas in which collision has occurred, such as along the Saint Elias and Border Ranges faults, rather than the relatively parallel fault movement characteristic of the Fairweather, Denali, and Totschunda faults. Volcanoes are often associated with large scale movement of

crustal plates, and the volcanoes of the Wrangell Mountains are thought also to be the result of plate movements. In some places in the eastern Wrangells, these later volcanic rocks overlie and mask the collision zone between Wrangellian and Alexander terranes. That the Wrangell-Saint Elias region is one of the most active areas of plate movement is also suggested by major earthquakes that shook southcentral Alaska in 1899, 1957, 1964, and 1979. The 1899 and 1964 earthquakes resulted in major uplifts of more than 40 feet in some areas.

The Wrangell-Saint Elias complex contains the most spectacular and extensive array of

glaciers and ice fields found outside polar regions. Since uplift of the mountain ranges, glaciers have become the dominant sculptors of the landscape. At least three major advances and retreats of ice masses can be identified. There are 100 named, and an equal number of unnamed, glaciers in the region. Snowfields of Bagley Icefield, which extends into the Yukon via Seward Glacier, are more than 100 miles long. Malaspina Glacier, a registered national landmark, and Bering Glacier form the two largest piedmont glaciers in North America with a combined area larger than some states. Among the world's longest glaciers is 75-mile-long Nabesna, originating on Mount Wrangell's slopes.

Each glacier has its own character; some are advancing, others receding, probably most are stable. For beauty, few glaciers surpass Russell, which flows from the slopes of the University Range. Rock debris scoured from valley walls during glacial movement forms moraines. For symmetry of moraines formed when tributaries of a glacier join the main stream, few glaciers can compete with Barnard and its many side glaciers. However, those glaciers which calve into the sea generate the most excitement for fortunate observers. Nowhere is this spectacle more concentrated than in Icy Bay, between Cape Yakataga and Malaspina Glacier on the Gulf of Alaska coast. At Icy Bay, itself formed by past glacial movement, Guyot; Tyndall; and Yahtse glaciers are actively receding and producing a steady flow of ice into the bay for several miles from the ice front.

Glacier-dammed lakes are common, and occur in areas where major glaciers flow past mouths of valleys not presently occupied by tributary glaciers. Some of these lakes empty on an annual basis through subglacial chan-

nels; others seem to be more permanent and empty only intermittently. One of the best known glacier-dammed lakes is Hidden Creek Lake north of McCarthy. Dammed by Kennicott Glacier, the lake empties abruptly through a nearly 10-mile-long subglacial channel to cause an outburst flood that is sometimes known as a *jokulhlaup*, an Icelandic word for this phenomenon. Oily Lake, at the margin of Malaspina Glacier where it flows past the Samovar Hills, is known for natural oil seeps that occur on the lake bottom and sometimes result in a thin film of oil on the lake's surface. This lake apparently empties intermittently, as do some lakes dammed by Bering Glacier. ••

Opposite • *Many geographers consider Russell Glacier, which flows northward 26 miles through Skolai Pass to the head of White River, as the divide between the Wrangell and Saint Elias mountains.*
• GEORGE HERBEN

Left • *Oily Lake lies in the Samovar Hills where oil from a natural seep darkens the shore line.*
• GIL MULL, REPRINTED FROM *ALASKA GEOGRAPHIC*®

Overleaf • *Folded moraines create a dramatic pattern in Malaspina Glacier, largest piedmont glacier in North America. Mount Saint Elias dominates the horizon on the left; Mount Logan tops the mountains on the right.*
• WILLIAM BOEHM

Glaciers, wind, frost and water erode the Wrangell terrain.
• STEVE McCUTCHEON

Climate

A transitional or continental climate influences most of the region. Mountain ranges paralleling the coast block moist maritime air from the Gulf of Alaska and cause release of its moisture (primarily as snow) at higher elevations. Although snowfall has never been monitored, scientists estimate that some of the world's heaviest snowfalls, upwards of 600 inches, may occur along the crest of the Chugach Mountains and on Bagley Icefield.

North of the mountains a climate similar to much of interior Alaska exists, with annual variations in temperatures of more than 150°. At Gulkana in the Copper River valley, during the five winter months, the average minimum temperature falls below zero, with some temperatures below -50°F. Summer maximum temperatures at Gulkana frequently rise above 70°F.

Precipitation in the lower elevations of the Copper River basin is about 10 to 12 inches annually, with about 50 inches of snow. North of the Wrangells, where a secondary rain shadow occurs, precipitation drops to an average of about eight inches per year.

Because of the strong influence of the coastal climate, the average summer day — even in the interior of the Wrangells — is more likely to have low overcast, rather than sunshine. Clear, sunny days are a rare treat.

Climate of the northern sections of Kluane National Park is dry, with widely varying temperatures. Farther south the climate is milder and more humid, reflecting the influence of moist air from the Pacific. At Kluane temperatures range from 80°F in July to -60°F in January. Destruction Bay, north of Sheep Mountain near Kluane Lake, receives less than 11 inches of precipitation per year; Mush and Bates lakes farther south receive 50 inches per year.•

*O*vershadowed
*by the mountains
and glaciers,
but still crucial
to the overall
Wrangell-Saint Elias
scene, are the
region's flora
and wildlife.
Floral variety is
related directly to
climate and, in turn,
substantially
influences wildlife
diversity.*

Flora

The region's wide range of climatic zones and elevations has resulted in ecosystems representing three major vegetational subdivisions: northern coniferous, alpine tundra, and coastal coniferous.

Northern coniferous vegetation is most common and dominates interior lowlands. Along flood plains and river bottoms in well drained areas, white spruce stands are common in combination with balsam poplar, a transitional species. With increasing elevation on well drained areas, a mixture of birch, aspen and balsam poplar generally occurs. Throughout low elevations on poorly drained soils often underlain with permafrost, grow black spruce mixed with occasional birch and tamarack. An extensive shrub layer consisting of resin birch, Labrador tea, and willows often flourishes within these stands. Upper limit of tree growth in interior areas is between 3,000 and 4,000 feet.

Two types of shrub communities exist within the northern coniferous zone. Tall shrub thickets consisting of dense willows occur along streams and river outwashes. Dense, tall alder thickets are widespread on steep hillsides — particularly on southern slopes of the Wrangells where they often extend from valley floor to 4,000 feet or higher. Dense willow thickets also develop on slopes which have been disturbed by fire or avalanche.

Moist sedges and grasses form a meadowlike tundra which occurs between 3,000 and 5,000 feet on more gradual slopes throughout much of the

region. Low shrubs, such as blueberry and Labrador tea are also common. On steeper slopes, from 3,000 feet to the level of permanent ice, grow a few grasses and sedges and low matted alpine plants dominated by mountain avens.

Samples of vegetation characteristic of the coastal coniferous subdivision occur in coastal areas bordering Malaspina and Bering glaciers and in a transition zone along the lower Bremner and Copper rivers. Mature plant communities on well drained lowlands are dominated by western and mountain hemlock and Sitka spruce which combine under the right conditions to form dense rain forests. An understory of

Left • *Ovoid buds of glaucous gentians, making full use of the short boreal summer, grow rapidly up through grasses and crowberry. The pleated corolla lobes untwist, while the walls of the bloom show vibrant blues and purples in a texture reminiscent of blown glass.*
• RANSOM SALTMARCH

Right • *In many places, lava flows have created wide tablelands covered with extensive carpets of dryas. During early June, the first green leaves begin to emerge through the shaggy mat of the previous year's growth.*
• RANSOM SALTMARCH

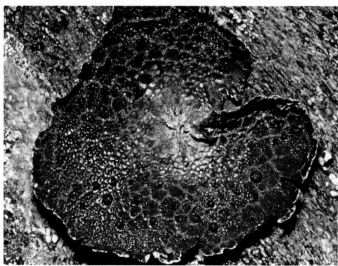

Far left • *A lichen known as rock tripe is frequently found on high rock outcrops. The lichen attaches to the substrate by a thin root growing out of the center of its undersurface.*
• RANSOM SALTMARCH

Left • *Labrador lousewort is a common plant of alpine tundra in the Wrangells.*
• RANSOM SALTMARCH

moss and shrubs consists of blueberry, devil's club and salmonberry. Timber line in the coastal mountains is about 1,000 feet. Above this point a dense shrub layer of alder and salmonberry exists. At still higher elevations a sedge meadow-alpine heath mosaic covers the land.

A cross section of vegetation occurs in the Saint Elias region, even though 60% of Kluane National Park's vegetated surface is alpine tundra. In the north where the range swings westward into Alaska, harsher climate limits the abundance and size of floral species. Farther south where moist Pacific air enhances growth, vegetation is luxuriant. The two climates combined nourish more than 700 species, perhaps the greatest variety of plants in northern Canada.

Below timber line the forest consists primarily of aspen and balsam poplar with climax stands of white spruce. Willow and birch grow in openings in the forest cover and willow and alder are common along streams. Juniper, bearberry, and reed grass dominate on drier slopes.

Above tree line — where permafrost is common in the alpine zone and occurs on north- and east-facing slopes in the subalpine zone — willow, shrub birch, and a short form of alder protect numerous smaller plants and flowers, including mountain avens and mountain heather. To the south, where moist marine air affects growth, common vegetation includes white spruce, grayleaf willow, buffaloberry, and lupine.   •

Above • *Instead of dropping from their branches at the end of the growing season, leaves of diamondleaf willow persist through the winter. When snows finally recede, the leaves reappear, colored bright russet, twisted and contorted by the rigors of the previous autumn.*
• RANSOM SALTMARCH

Right • *Catkins of least willow rise only an inch above the soil. Eventually the catkins will open and the wind will scatter their downy fruit across the tundra.*
• RANSOM SALTMARCH

Wildlife

Variability of wildlife reflects the diversity of habitats that exist throughout the Wrangell-Saint Elias area. Compared with temperate regions where vegetation is more abundant, the ability of land here to support large numbers of animals is low and limits the population of each wildlife species.

Dall sheep are the wildlife symbol of this mountain wilderness, a pioneering species able to occupy repeatedly glaciated areas and survive on low quality forage better than any other. Some 10,000 sheep are present in the Alaska portion of the region, primarily in alpine tundra of northern and southern slopes of the Wrangells, and to a lesser degree on northern slopes of the eastern Chugach Mountains. An additional 5,000 sheep occur in the Saint Elias range of the Yukon, being most common in the northern half of Kluane and diminishing in number toward the southern boundary.

Most sheep occur in compact herds, separated from other herds by topographic divides or lowlands. During summer, the animals occupy relatively large areas of alpine meadows and slopes between 4,000 and 6,000 feet. By early November, sheep begin to congregate on winter ranges, windswept areas where forage is available throughout the winter. A herd occupying many square miles of summer habitat may be restricted to a winter range of relatively few acres, which in turn influences herd size.

Mountain goats, less numerous and less widespread in the region than Dall sheep, are most abundant in mountains

A Dall sheep ewe protects her lamb in the Wrangells. Young are born in late May or early June; ewes normally bear a single offspring but twins do occur.
• GEORGE WUERTHNER

adjacent to the gulf coast, and in ranges of Kluane National Park where about 850 goats are found, the northernmost extension of this species in Canada. With onset of winter snows — which are generally heavier in coastal habitats — goats, like sheep, move to rocky, wind-blown ranges where forage is available.

Caribou from three herds inhabit the western and northern slopes of the Wrangells in alpine tundra and open spruce forests between 2,000 and 5,000 feet. The Mentasta herd grazes on north-western slopes of the range and head-waters of the Copper River, and calves on lower slopes of Mount Sanford and Mount Drum. Herd size has been stable and has been estimated at between 2,000 and 3,000 animals during the past 15 years.

The Chisana caribou herd occupies upper Beaver Creek and Chisana River drainages eastward to the Canadian border. This small herd (estimates run between 1,000 and 2,000 animals) seems to be nonmigratory. No tradi-tional calving grounds are known.

Caribou from the Nelchina herd, a large group which has undergone dynamic population fluctuations over past decades, occasionally winter on northwestern slopes of the Wrangells where they intermingle with members of the Mentasta herd.

A small band of caribou sometimes grazes in Kluane National Park and an occasional report of mule deer has come from the area.

Moose occur in several distinct sub-groups throughout the region's lower elevations where food and cover are suitable. Prior to the 1900s, moose were relatively scarce. However, land clearing for homesteads, and fires associated with this activity and with the Copper River & Northwestern Railway created favorable habitat. This, combined with predator control, caused populations to expand. By the 1950s, moose were con-

Far left • *Mountain goats, actually members of the antelope family, prefer the most rugged terrain. This pair scampers across rocky slopes of the Wrangell Mountains.*
• C. M. MOLENAAR

Left • *Both bull (shown here) and cow caribou carry antlers which are shed and regrown annually.*
• GEORGE WUERTHNER

Left • *Three wolves roam the Kaskawulsh River valley in Kluane National Park.*
• W. J. SCHICK, COURTESY OF PARKS CANADA

Below • *A moose makes its way through fresh snow near the Richardson Highway which borders the Wrangell Mountain area.*
• CHRISTINE TAYLOR

sidered to be abundant on all south-central Alaska ranges. Since the 1950s, however, populations have markedly declined regionwide and numbers are now one third to two thirds reduced from levels of a decade ago. Habitat change as a result of fire suppression, decline of predator control programs, and a substantial increase in sport hunting pressure have all contributed to the decline.

A wild herbivore not generally associated with the region is the bison. Two herds exist in the central Wrangells. The Copper River group first was established by a transplant of 17 bison to Nabesna Road in 1950. This herd since has established a home range between Dadina and Chetaslina rivers and in spring, 1980 numbered more than 82. Restricted hunting of this group has occurred since 1964. Animals transplanted to the Chitina River area in 1963-1964 form the nucleus for a second herd of bison that has established itself along bars of the upper Chitina River,

When summer stretches into fall, tundra berries provide an ample food resource for omnivorous grizzly bears.
• HELEN RHODE

principally around Goat Island. This herd numbered about 49 in spring, 1980 and has been hunted on a limited basis since 1976.

Habitat for bison, particularly on the upper Chitina River, is not widespread and this limited range has generated concern over the ability of existing habitat to support and withstand use by an introduced species. Through 1978, state harvest policies have been directed at keeping the herds stable, however, habitat deterioration, because of grazing and trampling, is evident in both areas.

Brown/grizzly bear and black bear roam throughout the Wrangell-Saint Elias area including forelands of Malaspina Glacier. An estimated 250 grizzlies, roughly one grizzly for every ten square miles, inhabits unglaciated borderlands in Kluane. Wolf and wolverine also are present although little is known about their numbers or habits.

A wide variety of smaller mammals — coyote, red fox, arctic ground squirrel, lynx, beaver, land otter, muskrat, mink, marmot, snowshoe hare — inhabit the lower slopes and lowlands.

Other than the Copper River system which supports major runs of sockeye (red) and a lesser run of king salmon, as well as silvers, pinks, and dogs, stream fish in the region are limited to a few clear water streams of the Hanagita and Beaver Creek drainages. Grayling, and in the Hanagita, rainbow trout and steelhead are most common.

Several deep, clear, cold water lakes north of the Wrangells — Tanada, Copper, Ptarmigan, and Rock lakes in particular — support good populations of lake trout, grayling, and ling cod. Shallower lakes of the Chitina valley and Hanagita drainage support rainbow and grayling.

As in the Wrangells, the majority of streams in Kluane are glacially fed and silty, and many small ponds are either too shallow or are deficient in vegetation and small animal life necessary to support fish. Most fish therefore are restricted to major lakes and their drainages: Mush Lake, Bates Lake, and Kathleen Lakes, all of which have abundant lake trout, grayling, and round whitefish.

Landlocked salmon, known as kokanee, ranks as perhaps the most unusual wildlife species in Kluane. This dwarfed variety of sockeye salmon had its migration route to the ocean via the Alsek River blocked by an advance of Lowell Glacier. Today kokanee spawn in Sockeye Lake which drains into Kathleen Lakes. Dolly Varden are found only in Alder Creek drainage east of Mush Lake.

No bird species counts are available for the Wrangells but at least 180 species of birds have been observed within or near Kluane National Park. Here, the lakes provide necessary requirements for several species of water birds including merganser, harlequin duck, scoter and common and arctic loon.

The Slims River delta serves as an important staging area for migrating geese and ducks. Flocks of snow geese gather here with sandhill cranes and a variety of shorebirds.

Subalpine scrub vegetation found throughout the Wrangells and Kluane provides favorable habitat for several species of ptarmigan, the whimbrel, golden plover, and Smith's longspur. Particularly noteworthy in Kluane are high concentrations of birds of prey, such as golden eagles, peregrine falcons and gyrfalcons. •

Ptarmigan occur throughout the Wrangell-Saint Elias area. The white-tailed ptarmigan (shown here in winter plumage) is distinguished by its all-white tail in both summer and winter plumage.
• JOHN C. PITCHER

Above • *Lynx have gray fur mixed with brown. Their long legs and fluffy hair make the lynx seem larger than it really is. Adults vary in weight from 15 to 35 pounds, occasionally more. Tracks of the lynx are outsized, for the animal has huge feet well adapted for traveling on soft snow.*
• R. CHAMBERS, COURTESY OF PARKS CANADA

Left • *Arctic ground squirrels share a tidbit. These small mammals are popular food for grizzlies, eagles and foxes.*
• GEORGE WUERTHNER

Region by Region: A Closer Look

Skiers approach Hitchcock Glacier in the Saint Elias Mountains. The Duke of Abruzzi, Italian mountaineer who first climbed Mount Saint Elias, named the glacier, presumably after the nearby Hitchcock Hills.
• MONTY ALFORD

The confluence of Root (left) and Kennicott glaciers is shown in this aerial from near Donoho Peak. The town of Kennecott lies just to the right of center, peaks of the University Range dominate the left background, and the Chitina valley extends out to the right.
• GEORGE HERBEN

Wrangell Mountains

Chitina River

U.S.
Canada

Saint Elias Mountains

Chitina Valley

The Chitina River valley separates the Wrangell Mountains to the north from the Chugach and Saint Elias mountains to the south and is the major access route to the south side of the Wrangells. The valley extends 100 miles from the Copper River to Chitina Glacier and is bisected by the Chitina River which taps water from all the major mountain ranges in the region. Numerous tributaries of the Chitina — many major rivers in themselves — including the Kuskulana, Lackina, Kotsina, and Gilahina, flow from glaciers through narrow, steep canyons draining the southern flanks of the Wrangells. Much of the valley floor is timbered, with white spruce, balsam poplar, and aspen dominating the well-drained areas. Black spruce and muskeg bogs are common in poorly drained environments, particularly those underlain with permafrost. A variety of vegetation, including dense, often impenetrable stands of willow and alder, grows on lower subalpine slopes of the Wrangells.

Mount Blackburn (16,390 feet) rises behind Castle Peak (11,000 feet) in the middleground. The peaks stand in the central Wrangells about 20 miles northwest of McCarthy.
• GEORGE HERBEN

The Chitina valley appears as a green belt rimmed by snow-clad peaks. The valley's immensity can be seen from a ridge on the Edgerton Highway, or from several accessible rises in the valley such as Nikolai Pass outside McCarthy and the ridges above Strelna, about 13 miles from Chitina on the road to McCarthy.

Human settlement in the Wrangells has focused historically on the Chitina valley. Following the roadbed of the Copper River & Northwestern Railway, a road extends 63 miles from Chitina to McCarthy. This route provides summer access to areas north of the Chitina River, but is frequently blocked by washed-out bridges or other natural barriers. Of particular interest to travelers on the road is the point where the road traverses the steel, single-lane bridge spanning a 200-foot-deep gorge on the Kuskulana River. Built in 1911 for the railroad, and possessing only rudimentary guard rails, this bridge inevitably causes trepidation among first-time travelers. Motorists cannot drive into McCarthy but must leave their cars on the far side of Kennicott River and pull themselves across the river on cables.

Far left • *Although the Wrangells are famous for peaks higher than 14,000 feet, smaller peaks and ice fields nevertheless portray the rugged nature of the area north of McCarthy. East of 16,390-foot Mount Blackburn rise summits forming the Rime-Atna-Parka peaks system, source of Kennicott and Root glaciers, the Kennicott River, and Stairway Icefall.*
• JIM VICKERY

Center • *Hikers enjoy this view of the Chitina River which flows 112 miles from Chitina Glacier to the Copper River. The river valley serves as the major access corridor for the southern flanks of the Wrangells.*
• DARRYL L. FISH

Left • *Winter snows brighten downtown Chitina, population 50. The small community, at the confluence of the Chitina and Copper rivers, is reached by the 33-mile Edgerton Cutoff from the Richardson Highway.*
• MATTHEW DONOHOE

Another mining road extends 40 miles up the Kuskulana and Kotsina rivers and provides good access to upper slopes of the Wrangells. Several roads in the McCarthy area connect the town of Kennecott and the Nizina River. (Kennecott Mines Company, which established the town, took its name from Kennicott Glacier, but misspelled it with a second "e.") Several homesteads historically have been established along the McCarthy road (Edgerton Highway) and lands have been cleared for agriculture, particularly at Strelna, Chokosna, and Long Lake. Today, probably fewer than 15 families live along the entire road.

McCarthy, at the mouth of McCarthy Creek on the Kennicott River, has a variable resident population that averages about eight in winter, and often three times that many in summer. The active, well-maintained airstrip with fuel service, centrally located in the Chitina valley, draws many visitors as well as those who use the town as a base of operations. A lodge serves transient hunters, prospectors, and outdoor enthusiasts.

McCarthy has a mystique which goes far beyond the mere numbers of persons living there or the old, gray, dilapidated buildings. Visitors to the town can gaze northwest to Atna Peaks (13,860 and 13,600 feet) and Regal Mountain (13,845 feet) which form a white wall more than 13,000 feet high. The community comes across as a special place, quiet and removed from everyday reality — a place where one can become immersed and feel comfortable.

East of McCarthy, in the lowlands between the Nizina and Chitina rivers, stand the small mining camps of May Creek and Dan Creek. Once linked by road and a bridge across the Nizina River, the camps were active placer

Left • *The airstrip at May Creek, former site of a small placer mining operation, provides access to the mountainous terrain east of McCarthy.*
• GEORGE HERBEN

Right • *Aerial view of McCarthy and its airstrip; and Kennecott, on the upper edge of Kennicott Glacier. Spelling of "Kennecott" varies, but generally the town and mining company are spelled "Kennecott." The glacier and the river are spelled "Kennicott" after early Alaska explorer Robert Kennicott.*
• GEORGE HERBEN

mining centers. The 1964 earthquake destroyed the approaches to the bridge, but, before then, the communities had declined. Good airstrips are found in both places and about five families live in the camps year-round. Today, only Dan Creek supports an active placer mining operation.

Chitistone Falls cascades 300 feet from the upper to lower valleys of the Chitistone River in the eastern Wrangells.
• GIL MULL

Wrangell
Mountains

Nizina
River

Chitistone
River

U.S.
Canada

Saint Elias Mountains

Nizina and Chitistone Canyons

At the heart of the Wrangell-Saint Elias complex lie the Nizina and Chitistone river drainages. The area has great geographic variation, ranging from montane forest on the lower Nizina, through jagged peaks and canyons of the upper Nizina and Chitistone rivers, to lush meadows and alpine tundra at higher elevations. Local features, particularly Chitistone Canyon, amply show the power of natural forces to shape land over geologic time. The Chitistone River cascades 300 feet from its upper basin over Chitistone Falls into a narrow gorge which opens into the main canyon at the junction of Chitistone Glacier. The canyon stretches 20 miles from the gorge to just above the confluence of Chitistone and Nizina rivers and is extremely deep, its walls rising in some places 4,000 feet within a mile of the river. Numerous waterfalls cascade down the canyon walls. Chitistone Gorge resembles Yellowstone Canyon with brightly colored, serrated walls rising above a narrow, rock-strewn river bed.

Right •
Limestone cliffs rise more than 4,000 feet above the valley floor in the Chitistone Canyon.
• GEORGE HERBEN

Below • *Parched mud starkly contrasts with storm clouds over the Chitistone valley in the eastern Wrangells. Chitistone Canyon, whose walls rise 4,000 feet within a mile of the river, extends 20 miles from Chitistone Gorge to just above the confluence of the Chitistone and Nizina rivers.*
• DAVID FRITTS

Left • *A rock glacier creeps ever so slowly down a side valley toward the Chitistone River.*
• GEORGE HERBEN

Below • *Folded sediments along Nizina River testify to the strength of geological forces shaping the earth's crust.*
• GIL MULL

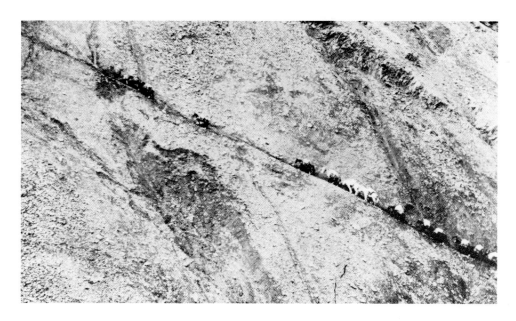

An early (**left**) and contemporary (**right**) view of the historic Goat Trail through the Wrangells: Well-broken animals of the International Boundary Commission's survey packtrain climb the steep, narrow path out of the Chitistone River valley.
• REPORT OF INTERNATIONAL BOUNDARY COMMISSION

Hikers cross one of many side drainages along The Trail originally pioneered by Natives.
• DEAN TROYER

Although much broader, upper Nizina Canyon is also very deep. Here the valley's west wall of light gray limestone rises almost vertically above the river. In places the limestones have been warped into broad folds; elsewhere, the folds become extremely tight. With a relief of 4,000 feet in three quarters of a mile, many sections are steeper than 70°.

Erosion of Nizina and Chitistone canyons has nicely revealed part of the geologic history of the area. Exposures show that limestones and other sedimentary rocks of the lower parts of the canyons were first folded and uplifted, and then covered by vast outpourings of lava and other igneous rocks that form the high parapets capping the mountains between the canyons.

Slopes of nearby Sourdough Peak (6,201 feet) contain some excellent examples of rock glaciers, slides of broken rock mixed with ice, that flow slowly down a slope.

The immensity and depth of both canyons are best viewed from rolling scree slopes of Nikolai Pass on the west side of the canyons opposite the confluence of Chitistone and Nizina rivers and accessible by trail from McCarthy Creek.

Winding through Chitistone Canyon, up the gorge and continuing over Chitistone and Skolai passes is The Goat Trail. Its use dates back to Athabascan hunting and trading parties. The trail is a natural path through the Wrangells, and Chitistone and Skolai passes form the only low point in the range. The Goat Trail was further defined by miners traveling to the Chisana gold fields during the 1912-1913 rush. The route is tremendously scenic, but arduous, particularly in upper reaches where it traverses steep scree slopes approaching Chitistone Pass. From the pass, the trail offers views to the northeast through Skolai Pass to the upper valley of the White River, and to the west to the series of peaks rising above Hole-in-the-Wall Glacier.

Mount Natazhat (13,435 feet) crowns a portion of the Saint Elias Mountains about 61 miles northeast of McCarthy.
• GEORGE HERBEN

Beaver Creek

Wrangell Mountains

U.S. Canada

Saint Elias Mountains

Beaver Creek Drainage

Beaver Creek valley and associated drainages extending to the White River represent topography typical of the northeast flank of the Wrangell Mountains where they merge with the Nutzotin Mountains of the eastern Alaska Range. Gentle topography, with small, often clear water streams, and a drier climate resulting in less dense vegetation, allows easier cross country travel than elsewhere in the region. The clear, deep waters of Ptarmigan, Rock, Braye, and several smaller lakes are set like jewels against the backdrop of the Saint Elias Mountains to the south. Access to these lakes is by floatplane or by trail from landing areas in the White River valley and Chisana. Mount Natazhat (13,435 feet) and Mount Sulzer (10,926 feet) dominate the view. North of Beaver Creek only light vegetation covers the stark, reddish-brown slopes of the Nutzotins. These contrast sharply with the

Vegetation covers the hills and valley of Beaver Creek near Horsfeld, between the Saint Elias and Nutzotin mountains.
• GERALD WRIGHT, NATIONAL PARK SERVICE

more gentle and richly vegetated alpine slopes to the south in the area between Solo Mountain (5,878 feet) and Wiki Peak (7,655 feet). To the north, the Nutzotins merge with the broad, lake-studded Tetlin Lowlands which stretch beyond the Alaska Highway and form a natural physiographic boundary for the region.

*Nabesna Road,
a gravel corridor
kept open year-round,
leads 51 miles from the
Tok Cutoff to the nearly
abandoned settlement
of Nabesna.*
• JOHN AND MARGARET IBBOTSON

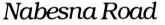

Nabesna Road

Lowlands north of the Wrangells extending from the Copper River headwaters southeastward to the Nabesna River are dominated by wet tundra and black spruce bogs. The Nabesna Road, which runs 51 miles from Slana on the Tok Cutoff to the Nabesna mine, divides the area. This road and the McCarthy Road provide the only good access into the interior of the Wrangells. This dirt road is generally passable during drier summer months. In the winter the highway department keeps the road open. Several families reside along the route where they guide, trap, and provide visitor services. Most residents congregate near Jack Lake. To the south Mount Sanford, Capital Mountain (7,731 feet), Tanada Peak (9,240 feet), and Mount Gordon (9,040 feet) dominate the horizon; to the north rise the lower, more gentle slopes of the Mentasta Mountains of the eastern Alaska Range.

Nestled in wet tundra south of Nabesna Road and separated from each other by a

*Mount Sanford
(16,237 feet)
rises beyond
Grizzly Lake and
Grizzly Lake Ranch
at mile 53 of the
Tok Cutoff.*
• ED COOPER, REPRINTED FROM
ALASKA® MAGAZINE

small, marshy isthmus are Copper and Tanada lakes. These large, scenic, clear water lakes are uniformly deep, exceeding 200 feet. They support an active fly-in fishing enterprise with a few fish camps located along the shorelines. Tanada Lake's outlet is seven miles from Nabesna Road and all-terrain vehicle traffic between the two points, uncontrolled in the past, has led to serious deterioration of a broad zone of wet tundra. Both Copper and Tanada lakes add to the headwaters of the Copper River which originates at Copper Glacier.

Ruins of Nabesna mine and associated buildings stand at the end of Nabesna Road at the base of White Mountain. Here miners worked an underground lode deposit that produced about $1.9 million in gold between 1931 and 1940.

Another major drainage of the northcentral Wrangells is Jacksina Creek, a large, fast-flowing, silt-laden stream which joins the Nabesna River near Nabesna. The valley at this point is covered with open, well-developed montane forest, dotted with small lakes in various stages of biological development. Jacksina Canyon forms a natural gateway to the extensive plateau country of the northern Wrangells. From above Wait Creek to Grizzly Lake near Jacksina Creek's headwaters are rolling scree slopes and alpine meadows lying between 3,500 and 5,500 feet. More than 1,900 Dall sheep, probably the largest concentration in Alaska, take advantage of the ideal habitat provided by the slopes and meadows.

Above •
*Jim Lowell
surveys an
unnamed
alpine lake in
the Bremner
River drainage.*
• GIL MULL

*The Chugach
Mountains
rise to the
south of Tebay
Lake, a source for
water draining into
the Hanagita River.*
• GIL MULL

*Wrangell
Mountains*

*Hanagita
River*

U.S.
Canada

Saint Elias Mountains

*Bremner
River*

Bremner and Hanagita Drainages

South of the Chitina River valley in the eastern Chugach Mountains exists a vast wilderness essentially untouched by human use. Bounded by the Copper River on the west, the Chitina River on the north, and large snowfields on the south, the isolated drainages have no easy access. Except for some small mining operations in the Golconda Creek area, human use is limited to a small number of fly-in fishermen and hunters. The Hanagita and Tebay rivers, tributaries of the Chitina River, are two of the few major clear water rivers in the Wrangell-Saint Elias complex. Each river, draining a deep blue lake of the same name, offers excellent fishing. For fishermen the clear water distinction is important because most rivers and streams in the region are glacially fed and their waters are obscured by high concentrations of finely powdered rock flour released by melting glacier ice. Thus the only clear water streams are those that do not have glaciers in their headwaters or those that flow from lakes large enough to act as a settling basin for the glacial flour.

*A rainbow
is created by bouncing
waters of a falls in the
upper drainage of Little
Bremner River.*
• GIL MULL

The Bremner River, a natural unit with glacial and mountain boundaries opening only at its junction with the Copper River, remains one of the last truly pristine watersheds in North America. Access to the river's upper reaches other than by helicopter is available only at a landing strip near Golconda Creek, and this area is separated from the river's main stem by the steep-walled gorge of Twelve Mile Canyon. The Bremner thus survives without changes brought by man from any age. Influenced by coastal weather patterns, vegetation representative of the coastal forest — hemlocks and Sitka spruce — occurs in certain areas of the drainage. The river's mouth is a major nesting area for trumpeter swans.

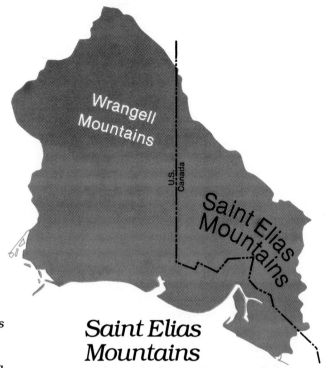

Mount Saint Elias looms above Icy Bay, a major indentation along the Gulf of Alaska coast that was filled with glacier ice at the turn of the century.
• CRAIG BERG

Saint Elias Mountains

Seventy-five miles east of the Copper River a relatively low pass crosses the mountains. This low area, occupied by the Tana Glacier, Bagley Icefield, and Bering Glacier, marks the western edge of the Saint Elias Mountains. Although the trail along this low area required crossing many miles of glaciers and snow-fields, in earlier days this was a minor access route, used by Natives and a few hardy prospectors, from the coast to the Wrangell Mountains.

To the east is largely a land of ice field and rock — a forbidding land, parts of which appear similar to Antarctica. An exception is the valley of Granite Creek, a tributary of the Tana River. Separated from the Bagley Icefield to the south by the high peaks of Thompson Ridge, this valley appears as a green oasis punctuated by tongues of ice flowing from the range's crest. The valley's lower end is blocked by the terminus of Tana Glacier, but minor recent recession has allowed waters of Granite Creek to carve a narrow gorge between ice and rock to drain Barkley Lake, a feature still shown on many maps. Upstream a few miles, the setting of Ross Green Lake, at the foot of Thompson Ridge, is reminiscent of the Grand Tetons. Although the valley can be reached by an arduous hike up the Tana River, the only ready access is by floatplane to Ross Green Lake.

Immense Bagley Icefield occupies a linear trench extending more than 100 miles eastward from Waxell Ridge and Mount Steller (10,267 feet), in the eastern Chugach Mountains, to the main Saint Elias range. Near the International Boundary the ice field is known as Columbus Glacier, and farther east in Canada, between Mount Saint Elias and Mount Logan, the ice field becomes Seward Glacier, source of most of the ice that flows out of the mountains to become giant Malaspina Glacier. At about 5,500 feet, Seward Glacier occupies a giant bowl surrounded by some of the highest peaks of the range.

Mount Saint Elias (18,008 feet), rising from near tidewater, has been a major landmark since Commander Vitus Bering sighted it in 1741 from far out to sea. The peak's distinctive pyramid shape led Bering and others to classify it as a volcano. This myth was not dispelled until 150 years after Bering's first sighting.

Mount Logan (19,850 feet) is 1,842 feet

higher than Saint Elias and only 470 feet lower than Mount McKinley, North America's highest peak. In terms of sheer bulk, Logan has no rival. Viewed from either the north or south, this massif appears as a long ridge, which actually is a rounded plateau. For 13 miles the ridge exceeds 17,500 feet. In spite of its height and bulk, Logan, isolated in the center of ice and lower peaks, was not named or recognized as a major peak until 1891. While climbing in the area in 1890, and again in 1891, I.C. Russell named the peak for a prominent Canadian geologist. In 1891 Russell described the scene surrounding Logan from a 14,000-foot ridge on Mount Saint Elias:

I expected to see a comparatively low, forested country stretching away to the north, with lakes and rivers and perhaps some signs of human habitation. What met my astonished gaze was a vast snow-covered region, limitless in expanse, through which hundreds, perhaps thousands, of bare, angular mountain peaks projected. There was not a stream, not a lake, and not a vestige of vegetation of any kind in sight. A more desolate or utterly lifeless land one never beheld. Vast, smooth, snow surfaces without crevasses stretched away to limitless distances, broken only by jagged and angular mountain peaks.

From a snow accumulation area on Mount Logan's north side, Hubbard Glacier follows a circuitous route for about 70 miles to tidewater at the end of Disenchantment Bay at the head of Yakutat Bay. In 1973 and 1974 a sudden advance — a surge — of this glacier threatened to block Russell and Nunatak fjords, which form the upper end of Disenchantment Bay. The ice advance finally halted a few hundred yards from Osier Island. Action of tidal currents past the glacier face continually undercuts large masses of ice that calve from the 300-foot-high face.

A major earthquake in 1899 resulted in beaches along Disenchantment Bay being uplifted more than 40 feet.
• GIL MULL, REPRINTED FROM *ALASKA GEOGRAPHIC®*

Left • *The front of Hubbard Glacier reaches the ocean at Disenchantment Bay. The spit connecting the island with the mainland shown in this 1946 photo no longer exists.*
• C. M. MOLENAAR

Below • *Eighty-mile-long Hubbard Glacier offers spectacular views of calving ice to fortunate viewers.*
• GIL MULL

A boat about 60 feet long approaches the face of Nunatak Glacier at Nunatak Fjord near Yakutat.
• C. M. MOLENAAR

South of Disenchantment Bay to the Alsek River the mountains become lower and are separated by large expanses of snowfields and glaciers. Occasional green vegetated hillsides stand out in stark contrast. In this area, West Nunatak and Novatak glaciers occupy the trench of Fairweather fault, one of the most active in Alaska and the source of giant earthquakes in 1899 and 1957.

Flowing north and west from the head of Hubbard Glacier, Logan Glacier merges with Chitina Glacier near the International Boundary to form the upper end of Chitina valley.

In Yukon Territory, south and east of Logan, the Saint Elias Mountains cross Kluane National Park. The Kluane Range of the Saint Elias Mountains, generally known as Front Range, parallels the Alaska Highway, presenting a solid ridge broken only by a few river valleys. Average summit elevation in the Kluane Range is about 8,000 feet. Duke Depression separates this chain from the

King Peak (16,971 feet) rises west of Mount Logan and north of Seward Glacier in Canada.
• MONTY ALFORD

Icefield Ranges. Large plateaus alternating with a series of valleys, some of which contain glaciers, characterize the depression. In addition to Logan and Saint Elias, several other peaks rise more than 15,000 feet including Mount Luciana (17,147 feet); King Peak (16,971 feet); Mount Steele (16,644 feet); Mount Wood (15,885 feet); Mount Vancouver (15,700 feet); and Mount Hubbard (15,015 feet). Most of these peaks are in Yukon Territory, but some straddle the International Boundary.

Left • *A low sun highlights 10,070-foot Mount Seattle on the Alaska-Canada border.*
• CHLAUS LOTSCHER

Overleaf • *Lateral moraines form a sweeping pattern in the ice of Kaskawulsh Glacier which flows out of the Saint Elias Mountains and into the lowlands of Kluane National Park.*
• W. J. SCHICK, COURTESY OF PARKS CANADA

The Saint Elias Mountains are the source of the largest glaciers in continental North America. More than half of Kluane National Park is covered year-round by ice and snow. Most spectacular glaciers in Kluane are Lowell, Kaskawulsh, Fisher, Donjek, and Steele, all of which extend more than 30 miles from central ice fields to outer valleys. Snow accumulation up to 3,000 feet thick forms massive glaciers impressive both in appearance and effect on the terrain.

Surging glaciers, of which there are many in Kluane including Steele, Donjek, and Lowell, may move rapidly for short periods of time. Steele moved seven miles in four months in 1965 though it normally moves less than 30 feet per year. Surges of other glaciers have in the past dammed rivers, forming large lakes in valley bottoms. A surge of Lowell Glacier formed a lake nearly 300 feet deep and 50 miles long. This lake drained suddenly in 1850, sending devastating floods into Dry Bay on the Alaska coast. South of Kluane, Tweedsmuir Glacier surged in the early 1970s.

Kaskawulsh Glacier, which flows eastward out of the Saint Elias Mountains and across Duke Depression, divides the two major river systems of Kluane. To the north, water from the Slims, Duke, and Donjek rivers and streams farther north flow into the Yukon River. To the south, waters of the Kaskawulsh, Dusty, Bates and other rivers drain into the Alsek River which cuts through the Saint Elias range and reaches the Pacific Ocean at Dry Bay, 48 miles southeast of Yakutat.

The Slims River flows from Kaskawulsh Glacier to Kluane Lake, along the Alaska Highway.
• DAVID ZIMMERMAN

Opposite • *This hiker surveys the forbidding front of Donjek Glacier which flows northeast to the Donjek River in the Saint Elias Mountains in Canada.*
• W. J. SCHICK, COURTESY OF PARKS CANADA

Left • *The braided stream at the confluence of Kaskawulsh and Dezadeash rivers becomes the rushing Alsek River as it flows south to the Gulf of Alaska at Dry Bay, 48 miles south of Yakutat.*
• W. J. SCHICK, COURTESY OF PARKS CANADA

Sedimentary and metamorphic rocks deposited between 220 and 500 million years ago form the core of the Kluane and Icefield ranges. Volcanic activity millions of years later capped portions of the area with lava and other igneous rocks.

A belt of volcanic ash lies just below the surface in the Kluane area. This layer, averaging one inch thick near Kaskawulsh River, and four feet thick in the park's northern section, resulted from a violent explosion about 1,500 years ago. Scientists have estimated that the explosion cloud may have reached 90,000 feet. Geologists estimate the White River ash deposit, a result of this explosion, consists of about six cubic miles of material covering 125,000 square miles of eastern Alaska and southern Yukon Territory. The ash's source has been located in Alaska beneath Klutlan Glacier northeast of Mount Churchill. Ash is visible along the foothills south of White River, beginning at a point north and east of Mount Churchill and extending east into Yukon Territory. The ash can also be seen in road cuts along the Alaska Highway in both Yukon Territory and Alaska.

Far left • *Klutlan Glacier extends 40 miles east from Alaska into Canada. Scientists believe that at a site near the glacier a huge eruption about 1,500 years ago spread volcanic ash throughout much of the region.*
• ELLIS RODDICK

Left • *Alpine tundra — spongy bubbles of moss, lichens, and other small plants — makes difficult walking for even the most agile hikers in Kluane National Park.*
• ELLIS RODDICK

Below • *Visitors come to the Alsek River valley in Kluane National Park to study nature and enjoy a climate that is much milder than the climate of the park's northern sections.*
• W. B. LIDDLE, COURTESY OF PARKS CANADA

Right •
Haines Junction, population about 500, serves as the eastern gateway to the Saint Elias Mountains. Headquarters for Kluane National Park is here.
• GIL MULL

Above • *This peaceful scene welcomes fishermen who are attracted by good catches at the two Kathleen Lakes in Kluane National Park. The neighboring lakes are connected by a channel.*
• R. CHAMBERS, COURTESY OF PARKS CANADA

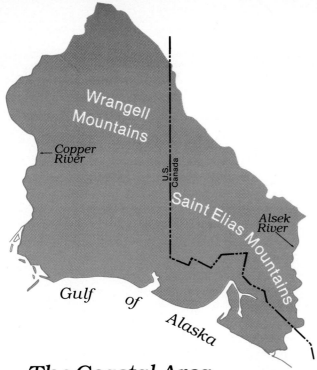

Wrangell Mountains

Copper River

U.S.
Canada

Saint Elias Mountains

Alsek River

Gulf of Alaska

The Coastal Area

South of the mountain barrier, and extending from the Copper River delta east and south to beyond the Alsek River, lies a discontinuous, narrow coastal plain. This narrow band consists of long, sandy beaches that in many places are backed by nearly impenetrable coastal rain forest. Sitka spruce, hemlock, and dense undergrowth of alder and devil's club mantle old beach ridges and other better-drained areas. These timbered areas are broken by marshy openings in the forest canopy and, near the margins of Bering and Malaspina glaciers, by broad outwash plains covered only with high grass. On rare, clear days, these open areas afford spectacular views of the white wall of mountains to the north.

The coastal plain and adjacent areas are underlain by unaltered but strongly folded sedimentary rocks that contain coal and petroleum source beds. At the plain's western end, just east of the Copper River delta, stands the abandoned townsite of Katalla, the focus for active exploration for coal and oil in the early 20th century. The town was promoted as an entryway to the Interior, and several railroad companies began construction of road grades to coal fields and toward the Copper River. These endeavors were dashed in 1906 when President Theodore Roosevelt, by executive decree, withdrew from entry all the coal lands in Alaska, and after the lands were reopened in 1914, the economics were not favorable for development of the coal fields.

This action, and the discovery that Katalla Bay was too unprotected to provide a secure port, halted coal development and also railroad building. A small oil field and refinery at Katalla, however, provided an economic base until the 1930s, supplying part of local fuel needs.

Between the Katalla area and Cape Yakataga, the piedmont lobe of Bering Glacier fans out over much of the coastal plain. The glacier's surface is marked by sinuous traces of highly deformed moraines, primarily of dark rock scoured from mountain cliffs by various tributary glaciers. Around the margin of Bering Glacier lie a number of lakes fed by melting ice; in other areas recent glacier recession gives a feeling of how the mid-continent of Canada and the United States must have appeared as the continental ice sheets of the Ice Age retreated 10,000 years ago.

Rugged slopes characterize the Suckling Hills, which extend for 10 miles near the 1950 terminus of Bering Glacier. The hills were named for nearby Cape Suckling, which honors Maurice Suckling, Comptroller of the Royal Navy in England during the time of Captain James Cook's 1778 voyage.
• BRUCE MOLNIA

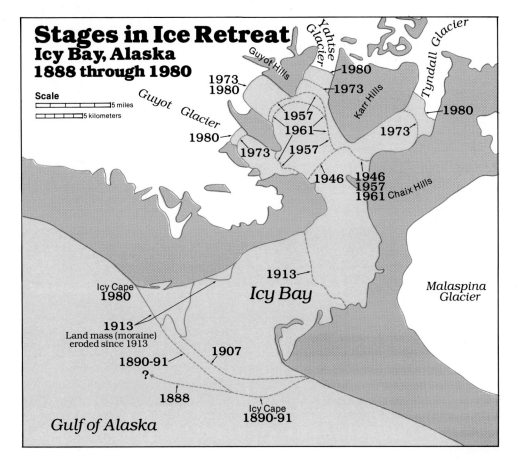

Stages in Ice Retreat
Icy Bay, Alaska
1888 through 1980

Scale
5 miles
5 kilometers

Guyot Glacier

Guyot Hills

Yahtse Glacier

Tyndall Glacier

1973
1980

1980

1980

1973

Karr Hills

1957

1961

1980

1980

1973

1973

1957

1946

1946
1957
1961

Chaix Hills

1913

Icy Bay

Malaspina Glacier

Icy Cape
1980

1913
Land mass (moraine)
eroded since 1913

1907

1890-91

?

1888

Icy Cape
1890-91

Gulf of Alaska

At Icy Bay glacial polish and striations on recently deglaciated bedrock stand out.
• GIL MULL

Opposite • *Tip French surveys Icy Bay and Tyndall Glacier. Members of the New York Times Expedition of 1886, which came to the area to climb Mount Saint Elias, named the glacier for British physicist and natural philosopher, John Tyndall (1820-1893).*
• GIL MULL. REPRINTED FROM
ALASKA® MAGAZINE

To the east, at Cape Yakataga, gold-bearing beach sands provided incentive for extensive exploration near the turn of the century. In addition, a number of oil seeps in the Robinson Mountains, between Yakataga and Icy Bay, attracted interest. Several periods of active oil exploration have resulted, beginning with drilling of a number of wells in the 1920s, and again in the 1950s and early 1960s. Lack of success onshore pointed the exploratory effort toward offshore areas in the Gulf of Alaska where a series of wells drilled by major oil companies in 1976-1977 also met with failure.

With the passing of both gold and oil exploration, the village of Cape Yakataga slumbers now with only a few residents who value the solitude and isolation. Most activity in the area is confined to a small logging operation near Icy Bay.

Icy Bay, at the foot of Mount Saint Elias, is a major indentation that now extends more than 20 miles northward into the mountains to the ice cliffs of Guyot, Yahtse, and Tyndall glaciers. As recently as 1900, the bay was completely filled by glacier ice that projected as a cape into the Gulf of Alaska. The rapid recession of glaciers to form the present bay is well documented by maps dating back to 1888. Recession continues today. As recently as 1960 the three glaciers ended in a nearly continuous ice face, but they now are completely separated by rocky promontories of the Karr and Guyot hills. On a clear day, the view of Mount Saint Elias above Icy Bay, with its floating ice cakes, is one of the most spectacular in Alaska.

Right • *Lobes of Malaspina Glacier reach toward the Gulf of Alaska on the north side of Yakutat Bay. The ice mass, largest of the piedmont glaciers in North America, covers 1,035 square miles.*
• BRUCE MOLNIA

Far right • *Tweedsmuir Glacier in Canada flows out of the southern Saint Elias Mountains to the Alsek River. A recent surge of the glacier has formed a gorge on the Alsek which challenges even the most experienced white-water kayakers.*
• BRUCE MOLNIA

Between Icy Bay and Yakutat Bay the coastal plain is almost entirely covered by the giant ice lobe of Malaspina Glacier. Even larger than Bering Glacier, Malaspina reaches the coast at Sitkagi Bluffs, a promontory of boulder debris carried by the ice. Much of the periphery of this glacier is so completely mantled by rock debris and soil that large forests have grown up overlying the stagnant ice. The presence of underlying ice is only occasionally revealed in the walls of sink holes where more rapid melting of the ice below has caused the forest to collapse into the cavity. Malaspina Glacier also has visually fascinating swirls of moraines contorted by differential advance of portions of the ice stream flowing out of the Saint Elias Mountains.

Yakutat, a fishing village on the eastern shore of Yakutat Bay, is the only population center in the coastal area of the Saint Elias Mountains. The village, population about 450, is a center for sports fishermen who flock to the Situk River and other clear water streams that cross the coastal plain of the Yakutat Foreland. In this area of abundant rain, the U.S. Forest Service maintains a number of wilderness cabins as shelter for fishermen and hunters.

Southeast of Yakutat the only breach in the Saint Elias Mountains is formed by the Alsek River and its major tributary, the Tatsenshinni. Although the mountains continue on to the southeast, this river marks the southern end of the geographical Saint Elias Mountains. For much of its length the Alsek flows through high mountains and is partially constricted by the terminus of Lowell and Tweedsmuir glaciers. The surge of Tweedsmuir Glacier in recent years has resulted in a gorge with a stretch of white water on the Alsek that has been declared impossible to run by experienced white water kayakers. On the other hand, the Tatsenshinni, which joins the Alsek below Tweedsmuir Gorge, has become an increasingly popular route for rafters and kayakers. ••

Opening Up the Country

The Northwest Mounted Police barracks at Dalton Post, a major stopover on the Dalton Trail which ran from near Haines, Alaska, to the Yukon River. The post was closed in 1906.
• CHARLES BUNNELL COLLECTION, ARCHIVES, UNIVERSITY OF ALASKA, FAIRBANKS

The Saint Elias Region

Archaeologists estimate the first inhabitants reached southwestern Yukon Territory about 8,000 to 10,000 years ago. These people, descendants of Asian hunters who originally came to North America across Bering Strait, are ancestors of the present-day Southern Tutchone Indians whose original homeland extended from Kluane Lake east to Carmacks and then south to the British Columbia border.

Frequently these Indians wandered in small family bands. However, they did build a few settlements in the Saint Elias area.

Jack Dalton, entrepreneur and adventurer, established Dalton Trail. Here Dalton leads a horse outfitted with special shoes to keep the animal from sinking in soft ground.
• E. J. GLAVE COLLECTION, ARCHIVES, UNIVERSITY OF ALASKA, FAIRBANKS

Nesketahin, about a mile north of the abandoned gold rush stopover known as Dalton Post, was a major trading center between the Southern Tutchone and Chilkat Indians. Local Natives acquainted with the old village claimed that it had hundreds of people and had been occupied for centuries. When Jack Dalton and E.J. Glave reached the village in 1892, disease and warfare had seriously decreased the population. The white men estimated the population of the village at 200. In 1898 a Northwest Mounted Police census counted 100 persons. Many of these were massacred, while fishing, by a White River tribe from the north, offended by an earlier trading visit of Southern Tutchones.

The resource-rich territory of the coastal Tlingits influenced considerably Southern Tutchone lifestyle. Tlingits controlled the inflow of goods into the interior and traded for the catch of Tutchone hunting and fishing parties. Before the white men's trading vessels arrived at the coast, Tutchones traded copper, hides, and fur for eulachon oil, blankets, dye, clams, and seaweed. Southern Tutchones traveled freely down the Alsek River to trade with the Tlingits at Dry Bay. This commerce peaked between 1840 and 1870. Although foreigners had reached the Tlingit villages on the coast by the mid-1700s, Tlingits wanted to maintain control of trading and refused to allow the outsiders to cross their territory to deal directly with the Southern Tutchone. Jack Dalton pierced this shield in 1890, and eight years later the rush to the Klondike completely overran the Tlingit trading barrier. According to records in Kluane National Park files, "As late as 1890 Natives in the area had still never seen a white man even though their technology had been influencing the Natives for years. The town of Haines Junction still has residents who remember when the first white man arrived.''

In 1902 a trading post was established at Champagne, along what is now the Alaska Highway, to accommodate Natives and miners seeking gold near Kluane Lake. When Northwest Mounted Police closed their operations at Dalton Post, the Nesketahin Natives who relied on the post decided to move to Champagne. Of the old village sites and fishing camps, only Klukshu, on the Klukshu River where it crosses the Haines Highway, is still used today. Occasionally Tutchones do return to Nesketahin to fish however.

In 1892 Jack Dalton enlarged an old Indian trail from Pyramid Harbor, near Haines, to the Yukon River. Dalton hoped to take advantage of Yukon gold discoveries by trading and transporting of supplies and people to the gold fields. Dalton Post, on the trail 125 miles inland, included a store, a Northwest Mounted Police office and several smaller buildings. Dalton charged $2.50 per head of livestock, and $250 per man, for use of the trail to the Yukon River.

In 1898 the Reindeer Relief Expedition attempted to herd 500 reindeer up the Dalton Trail to hungry Dawson. Most of the herd starved along the trail, however, and only 114 reached Dawson.

Business along the Dalton Trail maintained a steady pace until diminished mining activity farther north curtailed the flow of goods and people. Dalton Post was closed in 1906.

In addition to the Klondike rush, smaller discoveries on creeks in the Kluane area kept mining alive. Shortly after the turn of the century, gold and copper discoveries drew some miners. Renewed interest in minerals

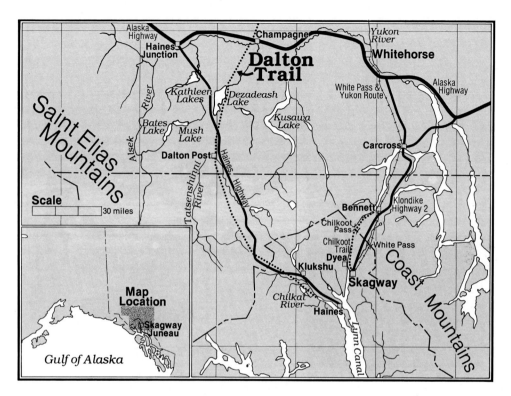

has led to sporadic prospecting up to the present day.

Construction of the Alaska Highway during World War II had a major impact on the Kluane area. The highway stretches some 1,500 miles from Dawson Creek, British Columbia, to Fairbanks, Alaska, and runs adjacent to parts of the eastern boundary of Kluane National Park. In October 1942, the U.S. Army Corps of Engineers completed construction of this overland supply route to Alaska. The road provided land access to the eastern Saint Elias area. Settlements grew along the highway and became jumping off points for expeditions into the heart of the rugged Saint Elias range.

The Wrangells Region

Early records for Alaska are less clear, but it is likely that the same aborigines who roamed southwestern Yukon Territory used the lowlands of the Wrangells at least temporarily. Since prehistoric times the area has been used for hunting and fishing, but because of the area's geographic isolation, few permanent settlements were established prior to the 20th century. Known settlements have been studied at Batzulnetas, just south of the Nabesna Road, and at Taral, on the east bank of the Copper River.

Prior to the 20th century, three major ethnic groups lived in the region. Tlingit Indians, occupying the coast at the mouth of the Alsek River, along Yakutat Bay, and west to Yakataga, were probably the most numerous. Marine resources were important to the Tlingit; inland hunting and other activity away from the coast were limited.

Two groups of Eskimos, Ugalakmiut and Tatitlek, occupied territory northwest of Cordova. Eyaks, linguistically similar to Copper River Athabascans, inhabited lands around the Copper River delta. Low population probably characterized the three groups, and their activities centered almost solely along the coast. Hunting and scouting expeditions undoubtedly explored up the Copper River, at least as far as the mouth of Bremner River, but these lands did not play an important role in their existence.

Athabascan Indians held sway over the interior of the Wrangells region. Small bands of Ahtna, or "ice people," ranged over areas principally within the Copper River watershed. North of the Wrangells, Nabesna Indians, closely related to the Tanana Indians of Alaska's Interior, had small settlements on the Nabesna and Chisana rivers.

The Copper River, the only water route across the Chugach Mountains in southcentral Alaska, had been a major access corridor to the Copper River basin and Wrangell Mountains since prehistoric times. Coastal and interior Natives, though separated by major cultural differences and by difficulties of traversing the Copper River Canyon, apparently engaged in at least limited trade. Copper had

Indian leader, Nicolai. Lt. Henry T. Allen visited Nicolai's camp on the Chitina River during his exploration of the Copper River and Wrangell Mountains. A copper mine named for Nicolai was located near the Nizina River in 1899.
• GEORGE HERBEN

76

W.R. Abercrombie, the Army captain who led the Copper River Exploring Expedition up the Chitina River valley in 1899, inspects produce in his garden at Valdez.
• ALASKA, 1899. COPPER RIVER EXPLORING EXPEDITION

served as a Native trade item at least 1,400 years before the white man's arrival, and copper implements were found along the coast by early explorers beginning with Vitus Bering in 1741. An early awareness of the copper's source was recorded in the English name the white men gave to the river, known to the Indians as Atna.

History records few penetrations up the river by Russian and American traders and explorers in the first three quarters of the 19th century, although a Russian trader, Klimowski, established a short-lived trading post near present-day Chitina about 1819. But in 1885 Lt. Henry T. Allen made a remarkable journey by ascending the river and exploring the upper Copper River area before crossing the Alaska Range to the Tanana River drainage. In his exploration he produced the first published map of the Copper River basin

and named Mount Drum, Mount Sanford, and Mount Blackburn. Allen pushed his exploration up Chitina River to the camp of Indian leader, Nicolai, and named the Chitistone River "on account of the copper ore found by the Natives near it." (Chiti is an Indian word for copper and is reflected both in the names Chitina and Chitistone.) Allen's explorations substantially narrowed the search area for the mineralization eventually discovered near Kennecott — the find that played such an important role in the area's history.

As a result of Klondike gold discoveries in 1896 in the Yukon, exploration up the Copper River and its tributaries began in 1898 with a large influx of prospectors and the efforts of the Copper River Exploring Expedition under command of Army Capt. W.R. Abercrombie. Attached to the expedition were geologists Oscar Rohn and F.C. Schrader of the U.S.

Geological Survey, who began to outline the major geological framework of the Wrangells.

With the aid of a map drawn by Nicolai, the copper mine that was to bear his name was located in 1899 near the Nizina River. The fabulous lode of Bonanza mine was located eight miles to the west on the ridge between Kennicott Glacier and McCarthy Creek in 1900. With these discoveries, the pace of activity quickened. From 1907 through 1910 the Copper River valley bustled with frenzied activity as the roadbed of the Copper River & Northwestern Railway extended up the river to connect the developing mines to the port at Cordova.

Finally, in 1911, the tracks reached Kennecott and for the next 27 years, until the mines closed, the Copper River valley was the main access route to the Copper River basin and the exit route for all ore from the mines.

After abandonment of the mines and railroad in 1938, the Copper River valley was quiet, except for a brief period in the early 1940s when the railroad tracks were pulled for salvage. Then desire for a road linking Cordova to the Alaska Highway system resulted in slow stages of repair and rebuilding of the abandoned railroad grade to become a highway that was to be known as the Copper River Highway. By 1964, reconstruction had reached beyond the "Million Dollar Bridge" between Childs and Miles glaciers when the March 27 earthquake struck, collapsing one span of the bridge and inflicting heavy damage elsewhere along the route. Once again slow reconstruction began but was halted in 1973 by court action. The issue of further road construction has not yet been resolved and the Copper River valley between Chitina and the "Million Dollar Bridge" is still silent. ••

Opposite • *Workers lay track near the end of the Copper River & Northwestern Railway at Kennecott, March 29, 1911.*
• E. A. HEGG PHOTO, ALASKA HISTORICAL LIBRARY; REPRINTED FROM *THE COPPER SPIKE*

Left • *By fall 1909, construction of the Copper River & Northwestern Railway reached Tiekel River at mile 101 north from Cordova. A few weather-beaten cabins are all that remains of a once busy way station at the confluence of the Copper and Tiekel rivers. Seattle newspapers dating from 1918, used to insulate the walls, tell of job opportunities in the north.*
• DAVID GRABINSKI-MARUSEK

Childhood Memories of Kennecott

By Inger Jensen Ricci,
Photos courtesy of the author

Editor's note: *Inger Jensen Ricci, now a resident of Anchorage, was born in Kennecott in 1918 and lived there until 1932 when she went to high school in Seattle. She returned to Kennecott for one year in 1936, then left to attend business school. Inger was at Kennecott the last six months before the mines closed in 1938.*

Inger (foreground) sits on a seesaw with a friend while her aunt enjoys the view from the lower swing and her father sits on the higher crossbar.

81

I am sure that I had the most wonderful childhood anyone could have! We had freedom that is no longer possible in our present-day life, unless one lives in a remote area.

The Kennecott I remember had a population in camp of about 300. I will have to explain the term, "camp." Our houses, school, hospital, stores, offices, power plant, machine shop, etc., all built to support the mill, constituted "camp." The mines — Bonanza, Jumbo, Erie, Mother Lode — were high above camp, one being on the other side of the mountain. Here the miners lived and worked year-round, some only coming down to camp once a year. When they did ride the tram down, they did not stop in camp, because there was nothing for them there, but took a taxi to McCarthy four-and-one-half miles down the valley. McCarthy had houses, a school and stores. But it also boasted several bars, two restaurants, and a red light district. McCarthy was off-limits to us, as children, unless adults accompanied us there. At McCarthy the miners spent their hard-earned wages in a very short time and returned to the mines to start again.

Kennecott was a company town. All houses were owned by the Kennecott Copper Company and were all dark red with white trim. The general store and the butcher shop stocked everything we needed. But if something was not available, we ordered from the Sears & Roebuck catalog. Rent and utilities were taken out of paychecks and books of scrip were purchased for shopping at the stores. We needed little cash, unless we were going to McCarthy. The company provided the school, books, and supplies. It maintained the ice skating rink in winter, put on weekly movies, provided gifts at Christmas, and did all it could to keep its employees and their families happy. The hospital was excellent, with a doctor, several nurses, and a good deal of equipment.

Camp had a very definite class distinction. Teachers; the doctor, unless he had a family; nurses; and office workers lived at the Staff House. The manager and superintendent had very nice houses. These were the upper class and they had a private mess hall.

The middle class consisted mostly of families whose menfolk worked at technical jobs and were foremen of various facilities around camp. Since my father was carpenter foreman, we were in the middle class.

The mill at Kennecott. The courts where Inger played tennis are to the left of the buildings farther up the slope.

The lower class included single men who did all manual and odd jobs and lived in the bunkhouse.

All houses of the upper class had indoor plumbing; some houses of the middle class did also. However, as the last of the houses built on the hill above Kennecott, our house did not have indoor plumbing. There were seven houses on our hill, four in one group and three in another. The four were large and had indoor plumbing; the three were smaller and had no indoor facilities. We did have running water until it froze in the winter. Then we carried water from the water house that was close by. Steam pipes were run all the way up to our house to help keep the water from freezing. These pipes were enclosed in boxes and one of our favorite pastimes during colder winter weather when we wore felt shoes, was walking on top of the boxes to see how much snow we could collect on our soles. Snow platform soles several inches deep would accumulate on the bottom of our felt shoes.

Our school had two classrooms. Junior and senior high school students met in the big room; students in the first through sixth grades met in the little room. About 20 of us attended school at Kennecott; another ten or

The Community Hall at Kennecott decorated for Christmas festivities. Note the dolls lined up below the stage.

so attended school in McCarthy. When that school closed for lack of students, the children from McCarthy came, usually by dog team, to our school.

The schoolhouse was the center of all activities for us. Sunday school was held there, and church too, when a traveling minister came up from Cordova. The ice skating rink was on the school ground and we skated before school, at recess, after school, and with our families in the evening. We had exciting hockey games

and races and only very cold weather kept us away from the rink. For a short time we even had a school paper.

Christmas time was exciting for us. Everyone had a part in the Christmas program. We prepared a play and many recitations long before Christmas and looked forward to Christmas Eve with eagerness and fear. All families and friends turned out for the Christmas program in the Community Hall. After the program, Santa Claus came and distributed gifts. All the girls received dolls. There was a huge tree, and candy and fruit for all. From the Community Hall, our family went to my aunt's house for hot chocolate and Danish pastry, and the singing of Danish Christmas songs. A Christmas gift that I have never forgotten was a dollhouse built in two parts, with one side open, made by my mother and father. One part could either sit on top of the other, making an upstairs, or sit beside the other. With Mother's help, Dad had made all the furniture, even tiny lamps with shades, upholstered furniture, bookcases with tiny books of different colors. The dining room chairs were covered with gay material. Carpet covered all the floors, and curtains hung from all the windows which had glass panes. Tiny framed pictures hung on the walls. I do not know how Mother and Dad kept the dollhouse a secret, but I was delighted to find it under our tree. Dad painstakingly decorated our tree, just as it had been done in Denmark, with tiny flags; paper roses; lots of icicles; and a few commercial decorations. We also had candles on our tree.

Camp had a volunteer fire department. Hoses were kept in many small buildings throughout the area. The location of the fire determined how the fire whistle was blown. I only remember three fires as I was growing up: one, around the stovepipe on our roof, was extinguished immediately.

Often in winter, snowslides blocked the tracks and prevented trains from Cordova from reaching Kennecott. One winter we had a pool to guess when the first train would get through; nearly three months passed before the train arrived. Some needed items were flown in once airplanes were in common use. Dog teams were the only means of travel in the early days. Many ptarmigans and rabbits inhabited the area around camp and my father raised rabbits and chickens, so we always had fresh eggs and meat. He built the chicken house over the steam line, so the chickens were warm all winter. We also had a root cellar where we stored all garden produce.

In winter, Sundays always began with Sunday school. In the afternoon we either skied or ice skated. My father and mother were beautiful to watch on skates. Coming from Denmark, they had skated most of their lives and could dance together as well on skates as not. They skied also, and started me early in both. Our ski trips took us up the mountains behind the mill and then down toward the glacier.

Another favorite activity was the weekly Saturday night dance. We always seemed to have at least a three-piece dance band, sometimes more. Everyone attended, including the children. We children loved watching the musicians and trying to dance. At the end of the evening, we ate cake the women had brought, and drank coffee and hot chocolate.

Another big, winter event was the New Year's Eve masquerade ball. Everyone came in costume and spent days making their outfit. My father was ingenious and he and Mother put together many prize-winning costumes. One time we went as a Dutch family and I still have the wooden shoes Dad made. He once went as a black mammy who had a front both in back and front, so it was difficult to tell if he was coming or going. But his very best outfit was a caveman. Dad built a cave beforehand at the hall. His costume was all of furs he had trapped, worn over long underwear. In one hand, he carried a huge club, and in the other, a dead rabbit. He won the prize.

The cooks in the bunkhouse aided us with

Chris Jensen, Inger's father, in his prize-winning caveman costume.

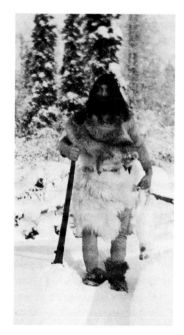

one winter sport. Two of us would climb the back stairway to the kitchen and ask the cooks for big pans for sliding. They never refused as long as we returned the pans, maybe a bit bent, but returned nonetheless. We had a wonderful sliding hill, all the way from the mill down to the store, if we were ambitious enough to walk back up. If the horses were going up, we would hook on the sled and get a lift.

Many games involved taking sides and searching for the other team after an hour's head start. Snow provided many good hiding places and often one side would give up looking. We had indoor games also and those

Mr. and Mrs. Chris Jensen, Inger's parents, with produce from their garden at Kennecott.

of us on the hill had signals with flashlights and colored paper to let the others know our plans.

Our community hall also was used for basketball games in the winter and everyone participated to have enough players. We followed boys' rules and often our games became rough and undisciplined.

Everyone joined in our baseball games. The ball field was the ice rink in winter; the field had been part of Kennicott Glacier at one time.

May Day was celebrated with a Maypole dance between puddles and small snow patches on the ball field. We lined May baskets with green moss and artificial flowers and hung them on door knobs of close friends.

A special treat was going on Dad's trapline with him. He was careful to have no human scent on anything. He also hunted mountain goats and Dall sheep. Dad's hobby was taxidermy. He had an owl stuffed and put away in the little cubby hole off our bedrooms and I would never go in there. Those glassy eyes staring at me from the dark frightened me each time I saw them.

Spring meant picnics and hikes. My father had one of the best of the many gardens in camp. He plowed it each spring with one of the wagon horses from the barn. These horses hauled groceries to us on the hill and one of our favorite pastimes, both winter and summer, was visiting the barn. At first the caretaker at the barn was an old family friend. Later a young man took the job. They both welcomed children who came to watch them milk, to play in the hay, or even to ride the horses around the barnyard. We were afraid, though, of the bull penned in the back of the barn.

Our summers, warm and dry, were filled with outdoor activities. Another good friend, a young ex-Navy man, Harold Glad, taught us to play cribbage, tennis, and even to swim. But the summer he taught us to swim, I had my knee in a cast from taking a bad fall while walking on stilts.

We had an excellent wooden tennis court way up beyond the mill. Sometimes we practiced with our tennis racquets at the handball court behind the schoolhouse because we did not want to walk to the tennis courts. After several games of tennis, we would head home and make lemonade, cooled with ice from the glacier. On extra warm days, we gathered on our lawn and kept the water going through the hose. A motley crew we were. Since we did not always have bathing suits, most anything sufficed.

In the woods, only a few steps behind our house, we built shelters. Our log cabin never did get any farther than shoulder high but we played cowboys there intermittently throughout the summer. There was a slight threat from bears but there were always several of us and we certainly were not quiet. Small black bears often were sighted, but were more frightened than we. Now and then a brown bear appeared.

One day Mother and I, with my Airedale terrier Pola, were looking for grouse in the woods. As we headed toward home down a trail near the dump, Pola began growling. Her hair rose on end. We looked back and found a small brown bear was following us. We had only a .22 rifle with us, as we seldom ever considered larger firearms. We kept walking slowly along the trail, keeping the dog beside us. It was difficult not to run. As soon as we reached the road, the bear stopped and watched us as we went on toward home.

Sundays were for hiking and we often packed our lunches and climbed toward the mines. Though we seldom hiked all the way to the mines, we often went as far as the two substations, Angle Station and Station III. Wild columbine, anemone, forget-me-nots, violets, geraniums, Jacob's ladder, roses, shooting stars, and now and then iris and lady's slipper covered the hillsides.

I enjoyed sitting high on the mountain and surveying the whole valley. Mount Donoho towered between Root and Kennicott glaciers. Beyond rose Mount Blackburn on the left, Mount Regal on the right. McCarthy lay to the south, nestled on the green floor of the valley with Kennicott River beyond.

Often families would hike one-and-one-half miles to John Letendre's home in the woods where he watched the camp's water supply. Letendre was a grizzled sourdough who had been a miner, construction worker, trapper, and prospector. He and his wife lived at Kennecott for years. From their home, another trail led to a favorite picnic site across the hill to a second creek with a dam where most of the water used in Kennecott was stored.

On other Sundays we would walk down the railroad tracks to McCarthy. We could buy ice cream cones there. At home we had ice cream if we wanted to turn the freezer, but cones were a treat.

Now and then my father's friend, Konnerup, would rent a car in McCarthy and his family and ours would drive out of McCarthy to a lake where we could fish or wade. Mosquitoes were more vicious at the lake and often we wore head nets. Konnerup ran the general store at McCarthy. He was a special friend of mine.

I had many special friends. My brother, 5, had died when I was 4, and everyone who came to our house was good to me. But I had special friends. Uncle Joe Wilson was one. He

George Flowers entertains his young friends at Long Lake. Inger stands at right.

from the peak of our house and every day the flag was raised and lowered. We had watermelon, a great treat, only on Fourth of July. Independence Day morning the children competed in races. In the afternoon teams from McCarthy and Kennecott played baseball. Baseball games went on all summer, during long, warm evenings, either in McCarthy or Kennecott. Sometimes the miners would send down a team. Following the Fourth of July game, we had a picnic with all the ice cream we could eat. In the evening there was a big dance.

During summer, tourist trains came to camp. We loved tourist days and made the most of them, gathering copper and bouquets of wild flowers to sell to the tourists. We enjoyed answering their questions, some of which we thought hilarious. Their clothing fascinated us also, and I am sure they were quite as interested in our casual attire.

In summer we would spend a week or two down the railroad line, either in Strelna, where we only went once, or Long Lake. Sometimes we went by speeder (small gas cars that run on train tracks); other times by train. At Strelna I first met Pola, my Airedale terrier, and fell in love with her. When her owners left Alaska, they sent her to me.

Several summers we went to Long Lake. One summer my parents, aunt and uncle, Uncle Joe and Louis stayed in the main log cabin. Fishing was great there, but we had to wear head nets most of the time. I even tried swimming in the lake, but the water was cold.

Other summers, Mother and I, with other mothers and children, stayed in tents by the creek at Long Lake. Old George Flowers, a black man who lived alone in an old log cabin downstream, entertained us with his guitar and showed us the best fishing holes.

never was without his cigar and he saved all the foil from them for me. We used to sell balls of foil for spending money. We mailed away the saved foil and received money in return.

Another close friend was Louis Eldeshope from Denmark. As the milkman, he took care of the cows and brought the milk by cart from the barn to the area where it was strained and bottled for residents' use.

The Fourth of July was always the highlight of summer. My father had erected a flagpole

A favorite summer jaunt took us to a mine near McCarthy, Green Butte. The Tjosevigs, friends of my parents, and Eleanor, their daughter, lived in McCarthy in the winter and at Green Butte in the summer. Mother and I spent some time there each summer or I went alone. Often other girls, from McCarthy and Cordova, were there. The second floor of the bunkhouse, a large log building with a big dining room and well-equipped kitchen, had several cots and we played there if the weather was bad. We drove to Green Butte in an old car and though the distance was not great, the drive took time because of the rough road and several tunnels along the way. In good weather at Green Butte, we packed our lunch and spent all day building towns in the sand of a nearby stream bank. In bad weather we spent hours sewing doll clothes on an old treadle machine or playing games indoors.

The longest trip we made each summer was to Cordova for a two-week stay with the Buhl family. They were from Denmark, too, and were close friends of my parents. Mrs. Buhl was an excellent swimmer and we swam in Eyak Lake nearly every day, regardless of the weather. The Buhls lived in old town, in a small frame house. The houses were built above ground, as often there was water beneath, and elevated boardwalks led from one house to another.

At Kennecott we had a little library in the building next to the bunkhouse. Mother was an avid reader and I, too, succumbed to the fascination of books. We went each week to borrow books. Often I know my mother must have wished she had not urged me to read because my chores were forgotten.

Fall was berry-picking time at Kennecott. We had our favorite spots to pick and never came back empty-handed. At Cranberry Hill, down the railroad track, grew cranberries, and mossberries which Mother used for pies. Currants abounded in the woods behind our house, and up by the dam. Currants were the hardest to pick because thorny devil's club thrived in the same area. Currant jelly was a family favorite, however.

Arrival of the traveling minister generated special excitement in Kennecott. Everyone welcomed Reverend Bingle, who came most frequently. He had a special way with children and usually attended Sunday school as well as regular church service. Reverend Kippenbrock was another who came several times for services.

I often went home from Sunday school and held church services with my many dolls, lining them up, reading the Bible to them, and singing favorite hymns. As I grew older, I played the piano for Sunday school.

My mother greatly enjoyed good music and played records on our windup phonograph. I especially liked to have her play them after I was in bed and could lie upstairs under the eaves and listen. My father enjoyed music also, and had a good voice. After supper, when the dishes were done, I would play old songs on the piano and Dad would sing — some favorites were "Annie Laurie," "Home Sweet Home," and Stephen Foster's songs. Mother joined in sometimes, but usually sat knitting. She could knit anything and took her knitting wherever she went. I still have a lovely maroon dress she knitted when I was in high school.

Those happy years, though long past, will never be forgotten, nor the dear parents and friends who made them so special. I am sure if the mine were still working I would still be there, helping my grandchildren to have the wonderful experiences that I remember so vividly. ••

Mining the Mountain Wilderness

Collapsed buildings are all that is left of Jumbo mine at Kennecott. Here miners worked the largest ore body (1,400 feet long) in the Kennecott complex.
• GIL MULL

Geologic and mineralogic research in the

Wrangell Mountains dates from before the turn of the century. Individual prospectors, small and large mining companies, early U.S. Geological Survey reports, and present-day investigations by that agency's Alaska Mineral Resource Assessment Program have contributed to public knowledge of mineral potential in the Wrangells.

Several types of metal deposits occur in the area. The most important type of deposit historically consists of bands of copper sulfide minerals concentrated at the base of the Chitistone Limestone along a narrow zone of the Wrangells' southern flank. Kennecott copper ore came from this type of deposit. Before mining stopped in 1938, Kennecott mines produced ore yielding more than one billion pounds of copper and more than 9.7 million ounces of silver. The largest ore body in the Kennecott complex, that of Jumbo mine, was only 1,400 feet long.

Because of the richness and high concentration of ore along this band, speculation about another potential strike of the magnitude of Kennecott continues. In 1977 the U.S. Geological Survey reported that a 25-mile-long belt may contain as many as seven undis-

covered ore bodies as large as Jumbo. Although the outcrop belt has been intensively explored and numerous small deposits discovered, more than 50 square miles of concealed bedrock thought to be favorable for copper have yet to be satisfactorily explored. Current exploration technology is considered inadequate to discover such concentrated, concealed deposits.

The most common type of metal deposit in the Wrangells seems to be large, low-grade deposits of copper ore associated with porphyritic igneous rocks. Potentially significant porphyry copper deposits lie south of Nabesna on the eastern side of Nabesna River at Orange Hill and Bond Creek. Extensive exploration of the Orange Hill deposits indicates significant amounts of low-grade molybdenum also occur there. Less important copper deposits may exist at Baultoff Creek, Horsfeld, Carl Creek, and Johnson Creek, all on the north side of the range. Two small porphyry molybdenum deposits lie at East Fork and Monte Cristo Creek in the same general area. Costs of developing mines in such rough terrain, and of transporting the ore from remote locations to existing smelters, are high. Questions of economic feasibility remain unanswered.

Principal gold resources of the area today

Opposite •
The Kennecott complex clings to a hillside in the Wrangells. Tunnels connected all the mines and ore was hoisted through the shafts at Bonanza mine and moved by tram three miles down the mountain to the mill at Kennecott.
• GEORGE HERBEN

Below • *In 1913, a brief but major rush following discovery of gold in 1912, brought several thousand people into the Chisana district (early records spelled it "Shushanna" and that pronunciation remains today). The district proved to be relatively* small, however, and all prospective ground was quickly staked. The best ground was soon worked out and Chisana quickly faded to become an isolated outpost with a few inhabitants on the northeast side of the Wrangells.*
• TOM TAYLOR

Above • *Ruins of buildings at Bonanza mine cling to the mountainside above Kennecott. Jack Smith and Clarence Warner, two prospectors, discovered the rich copper deposits at* Kennecott in 1900 by climbing Kennicott Glacier and nearby stream beds until they reached the Chitistone Limestone/Nikolai Greenstone contact zone.*
• GIL MULL

The mine at Nabesna, active in the early part of this century, is no longer operating. Geologists have recorded copper, silver, molybdenum, and iron ore, as well as gold, in the area.
• DAVID COHEN, NATIONAL PARK SERVICE

are believed to be contained as by-products of porphyry copper deposits near Nabesna. Additional disseminated gold deposits are known to exist near Indian Pass and Nabesna. Gold placers occur at Dan Creek and its tributaries, Chititu, Young, and Canyon creeks; in the Chisana area; on Kiagna River southeast of McCarthy; on Bonanza Creek; and at Golconda in the Chugach Mountains.

The exact number of mining claims within the U.S. portion of the region is not known. Wrangell-Saint Elias National Park and Preserve is believed to contain about 800 claims, of which fewer than 700 are bulk ore lode claims, primarily for copper, and the remainder are placer claims, primarily for gold. Most known claims are located on the south side of the Wrangells, with a few in the Chugach Mountains. Very few are active. The only known active exploration and mining in the area include Pandora and Silver Streak claims on the upper Kotzina River for copper, zinc, and antimony; copper exploration on Glacier Creek, and in Chitistone Canyon and at Orange Hill; and placer operations on Dan and Golconda creeks.

The Bering River coal fields on the south side of the Chugach Mountains near Katalla, have attracted interest since the turn of the century. Extensive exploratory work demonstrated the presence of high quality coal, but intensely deformed rocks resulted in high mining costs. A small amount of coal for local consumption was mined in the early 1920s, but the operation finally failed.

No potentially significant mineralized areas are known to exist within Kluane National Park. Where vegetation occurs, the land generally is underlain by Mezozoic sedimentary rocks of little mineral interest. The Burwash uplands north of Kluane are underlain by Tertiary volcanic rocks and do have mineral potential. This area was excluded from the park because of several blocks of hard rock claims. There has, in intervening years, been no activity on these claims and the feeling is that they are very speculative.

Burwash and Tatamagouche creeks in the Yukon have extensive placer gold claims, on which mining has increased in recent years. • •

Seeking the Heights

Climbers reach the top of 15,015-foot Mount Hubbard.
• CHLAUS LOTSCHER

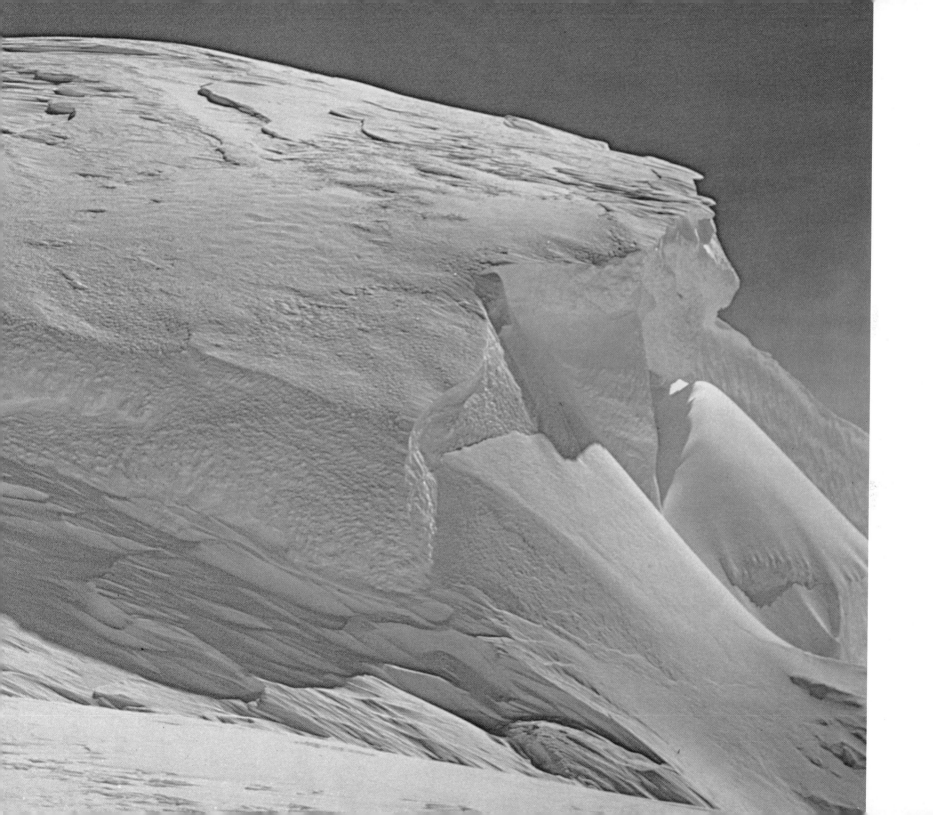

High peaks of the Wrangell and Saint Elias

mountains have drawn mountaineers for nearly 100 years. Because of their height and inaccessibility amid immense snowfields, conquering the region's peaks demands lengthy expedition mountaineering rather than shorter climbs typical of most North American mountaineering. Although these mountains are much lower than the Himalayas, their relatively high latitude results in climatic conditions comparable to higher elevations of that Asian range.

Early climbers focused on Mount Saint Elias because of its height (18,008 feet) and pyramidlike profile. The first attempt to climb the peak the Tlingit Indians called *Yahtsetesha* was made in 1886 by an expedition sponsored by the *New York Times*. An English expedition followed in 1888. Both were small parties that landed at the mouth of Yahtse River and explored southern approaches to the mountain.

The 1886 attempt, led by Frederick Schwatka, approached via Tyndall Glacier. At 7,200 feet, the climbers realized the summit was plainly beyond their ability. The 1888 expedition, led by Harold and Edwin Topham of London, first approached the mountain via

Libbey Glacier, which they named for William Libbey, Jr., a scientist, geologist, geographer, writer and soldier who was a member of the *New York Times* expedition in 1886. However, after discovering that this glacier heads at the base of a giant three-mile-high wall that drops nearly unbroken from the summit, they too turned to Tyndall Glacier. The party reached 11,400 feet on the ridge below Haydon Peak on the south side of Saint Elias before turning back. Benefiting from knowledge gained by these pioneering explorations, subsequent expeditions were larger, better equipped, and relied on other approaches.

In 1890, I.C. Russell, on a scientific expedition sponsored jointly by the National Geographic Society and the U.S. Geological Survey, pioneered a route from the head of Yakutat Bay to Newton Glacier, which provides access to upper slopes of Saint Elias's east side. His route traversed along the north side of Malaspina Glacier to cross Seward Glacier near its cascade onto Malaspina. During his exploration, Russell first saw and named Mount Logan, rising to the north across Seward Glacier. In all, this expedition spent more than two months exploring eastern approaches to the mountain.

I.C. Russell returned in 1891 and, like

Opposite • *Members of I.C. Russell's party rest on Libbey Glacier during their second attempt to climb 18,008-foot Mount Saint Elias in 1891.*
• U.S. GEOLOGICAL SURVEY, THIRTEENTH ANNUAL REPORT, 1892

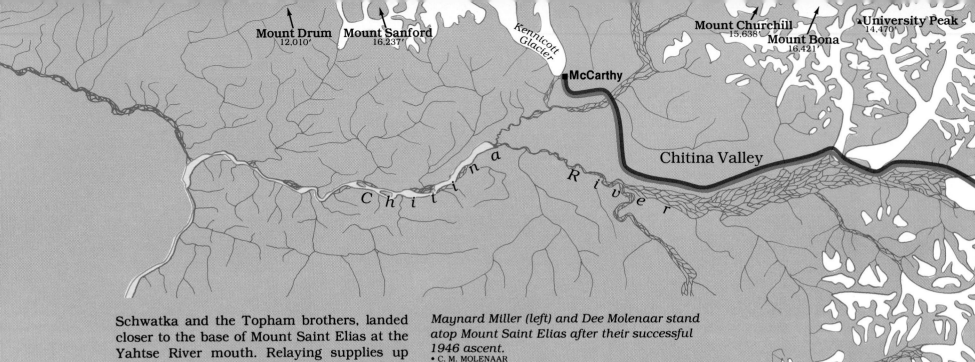

Mount Drum
12,010'

Mount Sanford
16,237'

Kennicott Glacier

Mount Churchill
15,638'

University Peak
14,470'

Mount Bona
16,421'

McCarthy

Chitina River

Chitina Valley

Schwatka and the Topham brothers, landed closer to the base of Mount Saint Elias at the Yahtse River mouth. Relaying supplies up Agassiz Glacier, he intersected his previous route up Newton Glacier and finally reached a saddle, that has since been named Russell Col, on the northeast side of Mount Saint Elias. From this point a broad ridge rises to the summit, but Russell was driven back after reaching 14,500 feet by a series of heavy snowfalls that resulted in extreme avalanching. Russell spent two months exploring the area. Although the climb was unsuccessful, he discovered abundant geological evidence favoring a youthful age for the mountains and also dispelled the myth that Saint Elias was a volcano — a misconception dating from Vitus Bering's first sighting of the peak in 1741.

Six years later, in 1897, two expeditions approached Mount Saint Elias. An American party climbing from the southwest was unsuccessful, but a very large Italian expedition led by H.R.H. Prince Luigi Amedeo Di Savoia, Duke of Abruzzi, finally attained the summit. The Duke's party included Italian

Maynard Miller (left) and Dee Molenaar stand atop Mount Saint Elias after their successful 1946 ascent.
• C. M. MOLENAAR

mountain guides and nine porters hired in Alaska to transport all equipment on sleds across the entire 25-mile width of Malaspina Glacier from the shore of Yakutat Bay to Seward Glacier. The successful route was that pioneered by Russell up Newton Glacier, and again nearly two months were consumed in the climb and return to Yakutat.

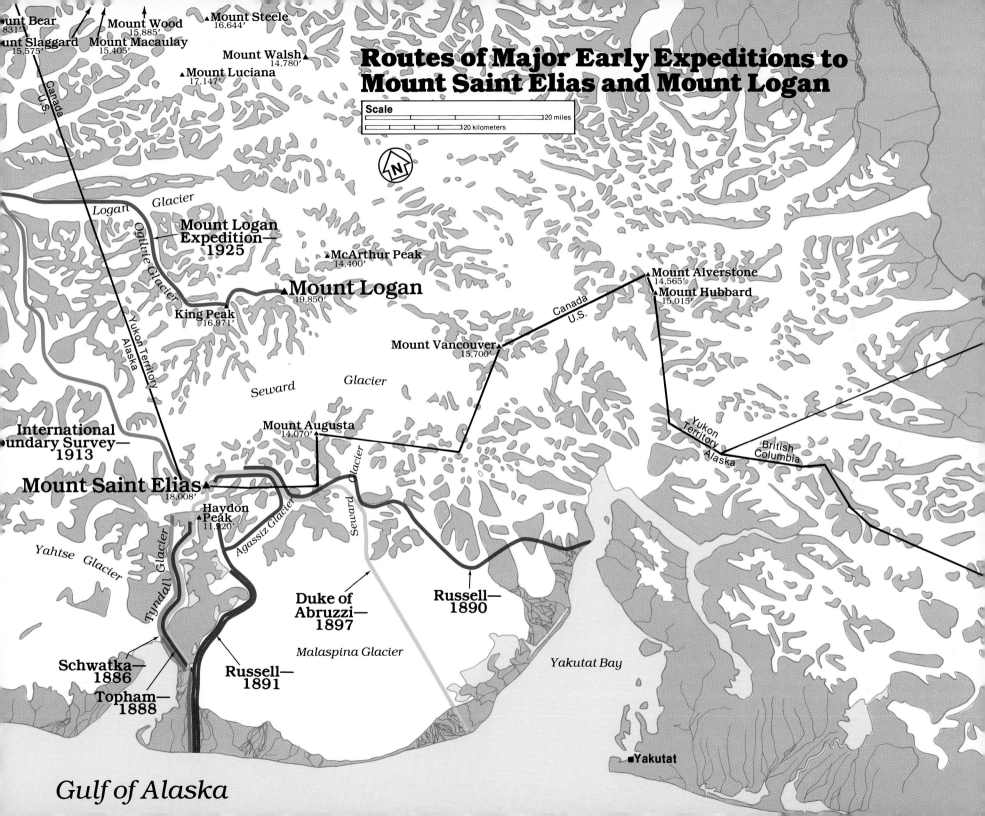

Routes of Major Early Expeditions to Mount Saint Elias and Mount Logan

Scale

20 miles

20 kilometers

N

▲Mount Bear
831'

unt Slaggard
15,575'

Mount Wood
15,885'

Mount Macaulay
15,405'

▲Mount Steele
16,644'

Mount Walsh ▲
14,780'

▲Mount Luciana
17,147'

Logan   Glacier

**Mount Logan
Expedition—
1925**

▲McArthur Peak
14,400'

▲Mount Alverstone
14,565'
▲Mount Hubbard
15,015'

Ogilvie Glacier

King Peak ▲
16,971'

▲**Mount Logan**
19,850'

Canada
U.S.

Mount Vancouver▲
15,700'

Yukon Territory

Alaska

Seward   Glacier

**International
undary Survey—
1913**

Mount Augusta ▲
14,070'

*Yukon
Territory*
Alaska

*British
Columbia*

Mount Saint Elias ▲
18,008'

Haydon
Peak ▲
11,920'

Agassiz Glacier

Seward Glacier

Tyndall Glacier

**Russell—
1890**

Yahtse   Glacier

**Duke of
Abruzzi—
1897**

**Russell—
1891**

Malaspina Glacier

Yakutat Bay

**Schwatka—
1886**

**Topham—
1888**

Gulf of Alaska

■Yakutat

Canada
U.S.

Supplies for the International Boundary Commission's survey parties were freighted up the Chitina River valley to remote points near the boundary where it crosses the Saint Elias Mountains.
• REPORT OF THE INTERNATIONAL BOUNDARY COMMISSION

After Mount Saint Elias was conquered, more than a quarter century passed before another serious mountaineering expedition penetrated the range's icy expanse. During this interlude, members of the International Boundary Commission, surveying the Alaska-Canada boundary between 1909 and 1913, traversed the area and climbed many minor summits in the course of their work. They also attempted to climb Mount Saint Elias from the northwest, but were thwarted by a combination of steep rock alternating with bare ice and, finally, by a storm that struck when the party was above 16,000 feet.

During the time the Boundary Commission was traversing the Saint Elias Mountains, mountaineering began in the Wrangells, now much more accessible with completion of the Copper River & Northwestern Railway in 1911. That summer, while most men in the area were scrambling for mineral wealth, Dora Keen made the first reconnaissance of Mount

Blackburn (16,390 feet) via Kennicott Glacier. The following spring she returned with G.W. Handy and several others. Keen and Handy reached the summit of Mount Blackburn on May 19, 1912, after 33 days. (See "First Up Mount Blackburn," page 108.)

After this climb, the mountains were abandoned to the footsteps of miners and big game hunters until 1924 when a reconnaissance to pick a route up Mount Logan (19,850 feet) was made from McCarthy. During February, March, and April 1925, in temperatures as low as -55°F, nearly 19,000 pounds of supplies were relayed by dog team up the Chitina valley and Logan and Ogilvie glaciers to the western foot of Mount Logan. In May the remainder of the largely Canadian expedition rode the train to McCarthy.

The expedition, led by Albert MacCarthy and H.F.J. Lambart, departed on foot May 12. From a base camp at about 7,800 feet on Ogilvie Glacier on Logan's northwest side, the actual ascent began. An icefall at the head of Ogilvie Glacier provided access to what has since become known as King Trench, a long, glacier-filled valley that rises gently from about 10,000 feet to Logan plateau, above 16,000 feet. The trench offered access to the mountain's upper slopes.

Violent storms twice forced retreat from 18,500 feet back to King Col at 13,500 feet. When the weather moderated, the party traversed the remaining six miles to the summit, which they reached on June 23, 1925. On the descent, a sudden storm resulted in two bivouacs without shelter at more than 19,000 feet, during which the entire party suffered frostbite. After another series of storms during the two-week descent, the climbers reached the Chitina River headwaters. Here they built rafts to float 50 miles downstream. The final leg of their journey required a 15-mile cross country hike to McCarthy.

This expedition remains unrivaled in logistical complexity and probably also in severe weather encountered; it succeeded only because of the members' determination and experience. Many years afterward, MacCarthy, one of the leaders, said he felt credit for their success belonged largely to Andy Taylor, a sourdough who had spent years in the Wrangells prospecting and guiding hunting expeditions. Taylor participated in the 1924 reconnaissance, organized the winter freighting trip, and then, with no previous high-altitude climbing experience, became a mainstay in the climbing. (See "Andy Taylor, A Man of the Region," page 107.)

Five years passed before climbing resumed in the Saint Elias Mountains. This time Taylor; Allen Carpe, another member of the Logan expedition; and Terris Moore made the first ascent of Mount Bona (16,421 feet) by an approach up Russell Glacier. Five more years passed before a 1935 party led by Walter Wood made the first ascent of Mount Steele (16,644 feet). This climb was the last recorded ascent of a major peak in the range in which aircraft played no part. Earlier the same year, a National Geographic expedition led by Bradford Washburn had demonstrated the effectiveness of aerial support in exploring Hubbard and Lowell glaciers.

In 1937, from his mudflat strip at Valdez, pioneer bush pilot Bob Reeve flew Bradford Washburn and Robert Bates in his Fairchild 51 ski plane to the base of Mount Luciana (17,147 feet) in the Saint Elias range. However, upon landing at 8,500 feet, the plane sank to its belly in slush. High temperatures and very little snow the previous winter had resulted in extremely rotten snow on the surface of the glacier. Five days later, after heavy rain and temperatures that reached 60°F, the weather finally cleared. Temperatures dropped sufficiently for a crust to form on the slushy snow, and Reeve made a dramatic take-off from the glacier for the return flight.

Conditions prevented Reeve from flying the remaining climbers to the glacier or retrieving Washburn and Bates from the glacier. After making the first ascent of Mount Luciana and a second ascent of Mount Steele, the two climbers walked about 120 miles down Steele Glacier and Steele Creek to the Donjek River and arrived at Burwash Landing at Kluane Lake almost a month after Reeve left them on the glacier.

The following year, 1938, Washburn and Terris Moore made the first ascent of the volcanic pyramid of Mount Sanford (16,237 feet), the first major new summit to be reached in the Wrangells since Dora Keen's ascent of Mount Blackburn 26 years earlier.

As war loomed in 1941, a party led by Walter Wood made first ascents of Mount Wood (15,885 feet) and Mount Walsh (14,780 feet). U.S. Army bombers parachuted equipment and supplies in support of the joint scientific and mountaineering expedition.

After the war, mountaineering interest resumed and, in 1946, turned again to Mount Saint Elias, which had not been approached since the International Boundary Commission's 1913 attempt. This time a Harvard Mountaineering Club expedition led by Maynard Miller landed by boat on the east shore of Icy Bay, formed by retreat of glaciers which had filled the bay when earlier pioneering climbs in the area were made.

The party approached the south side of

Left • *Haydon Peak (11,920 feet) looms above a climber on the 1946 Mount Saint Elias expedition. Harold Topham named the peak for Henry E. Haydon, Secretary of Alaska in 1888, and his wife.*
• C. M. MOLENAAR

Above • *Climbers approach the cornice summit of 11,920-foot Haydon Peak in the Saint Elias range.*
• D. MOLENAAR

Mount Saint Elias via Tyndall Glacier, following the general route of the Topham party in 1888. Aided by two airdrops of supplies delivered by Air Force Tenth Rescue Squadron personnel as part of a training exercise, the group spent a month establishing 11 camps and climbed Haydon Peak en route to the summit of Saint Elias. This second ascent came almost half a century after the Duke of Abruzzi first reached the summit. Almost three weeks were spent in the descent and long walk back to Icy Bay.

No major ascents were completed during the following two years but in 1949 Mount Vancouver (15,700 feet) first was climbed. This effort opened an era of great mountaineering activity in which major ascents were made almost yearly, including a number of first ascents of peaks higher than 14,000 feet. In 1950, the second and third ascents of

Mount Logan came within a few days of each other. An unprecedented number of first ascents occurred in 1951 as Mount Bear (14,831 feet), Mount Churchill (15,638 feet), Mount Hubbard (15,015 feet), and Mount Alverstone (14,565 feet) were climbed. King Peak (16,971 feet), the western tip of the Logan massif, and Mount Augusta (14,070 feet), 15 miles east of Mount Saint Elias, were conquered in 1952.

Left • *A mountaineer shows his rock climbing skills at the northernmost west ridge of 14,950-foot Mount Hubbard.*
• CHLAUS LOTSCHER

Above • *Ascending Mount Hubbard from Cathedral Glacier on the mountain's northeast flank.*
• CHLAUS LOTSCHER

Right • *A helicopter lands bundles of climbing gear on Alverstone Glacier in the Saint Elias Mountains in Canada. In the background rises 14,565-foot Mount Alverstone.*
• CHLAUS LOTSCHER

Since that time the majority of high climbing has concentrated on pioneering new and more difficult routes on previously climbed major peaks or on secondary summits. Some of these climbs have been epic undertakings requiring extreme skill and endurance. However, a few first ascents of major peaks still remained, including Mount Drum (12,010 feet) in 1954; University Peak (14,470 feet) in 1955; Mount Slaggard (15,575 feet) and Mount Macaulay (15,405 feet) in 1959; and McArthur Peak (14,400 feet) in 1961, the final major peak above 14,000 feet to be ascended.

In addition to major mountaineering efforts, important high altitude physiological and other scientific studies have been carried out in the area by the Icefield Ranges Research Project, sponsored by the Arctic Institute of North America and the American Geographical Society. These studies have dealt with long occupancy of a semipermanent camp established at more than 17,000 feet on the Logan massif. ••

Above • *Swiss climbers Heidi Ludi and Andreas Brun stand atop 13,905-foot Mount Kennedy.*
• CHLAUS LOTSCHER

Right • *Climbers survey rocky peaks on the flanks of 12,010-foot Mount Drum in the western Wrangells. Lt. Henry Allen named the peak for Adj. Gen. Richard C. Drum (1825-1909) who fought in the Mexican War and became a brigadier general during the Civil War.*
• THIRD EYE PHOTOGRAPHY

Andy Taylor
— A Man of the Region

Editor's note: *Many sourdoughs roamed the Wrangell-Saint Elias region: miners, hunters, guides, and those who simply enjoyed a one-to-one existence with nature. Andrew Morrison Taylor (October 17, 1875-May 13, 1945) was one of those early residents. Born in Canada of Scottish parents, Taylor left Ottawa for western North America at an early age. He captained a small launch on the upper Columbia River in the early 1890s but was drawn farther north by the Stikine River. In 1897, while a river pilot and engineer on a Stikine steamer, he agreed to take a sternwheeler to Skagway. Foul weather forced the ship aground but Taylor's salvage efforts enabled the crew to return to Wrangell. Taylor again set out for Skagway where he ran a string of pack horses over White Pass. By 1898 Andy had made Dawson his temporary home and for the next 15 years he freighted supplies, prospected and explored northwestern Canada and eastern and northern Alaska. During this time he became familiar with the White River country of the Wrangell-Saint Elias region. The following excerpt is reprinted by permission,* The American Alpine Journal, 1947.

But [Taylor] soon discovered his favorite ground, the White River, and came to know it and its watershed thoroughly. Thus he became valuable to the survey parties of the International Boundary Commission with which he spent several seasons as heliographer. He also handled their pack trains and supplied them with meat.

In the White River region he had several claims, and two cabins on White River, one on Rabbit Creek and another at Canyon City (in Yukon Territory), where he worked the ground from time to time. He first went to Canyon City about 1900.

In June 1913 Andy was on Bonanza Creek, a tributary of White River in what is known as the "Shushanna" country (spelled on the USGS maps "Chisana"). That year he was associated with William James, "North Pole" Nelson and a Mrs. Wales, who had come in the year before and built a cabin. Together they discovered important placer deposits and staked out claims. As they needed equipment, Andy and Nelson went out to Dawson during the summer, and word got out of this strike. A stampede ensued called the "Shushanna Rush." It lasted until the summer of 1914, and several thousand went into that area.

Andy returned from Dawson and worked his claim. As the gold field was developed, McCarthy in Alaska became the main base for supplies, so at that time Andy moved his residence to that

Andy Taylor (left) and his long-time friend, John Burnham of New York, in 1940. Burnham met Taylor in 1919 in the White River country and invited Taylor to accompany him on an expedition to Chukotsk Peninsula of Siberia.
• THE AMERICAN ALPINE JOURNAL, 1947

town. Most of the supplies were freighted from McCarthy by way of Skolai Pass. During this period Andy undoubtedly made many trips over this route.

Andy is said to have made and thrown away three "fortunes." He once came back to Dawson with a suitcase full of gold dust and nuggets (about $150,000.00). The first thing he did was to visit the bar of the man who had grubstaked him. Paid his debts, bought more supplies, then celebrated for a couple of days and gave away, threw away and spent his share of the gold.

After moving to McCarthy he alternated between working at the Kennecott Mines, prospecting on his own, and taking out hunting trips. Thus he came to know the Chitina and its drainage basin. His familiarity with this country made him the logical man to pilot the Mount Logan expedition on its approach to that mountain. •

Editor's note: *Dora Keen was born in Philadelphia, June 24, 1871. She attended Bryn Mawr College and was interested in public school improvement. Miss Keen traveled worldwide and in 1911 came north where, according to the American Alpine Club Annals, she became the first woman to climb in Alaska. In 1916 Miss Keen married G.W. Handy whom she met in Cordova on her way to the Wrangells. The following is excerpted from* The World's Work, *November 1913; reprinted courtesy of Doubleday & Company Inc. Photographs and map reproduction provided through courtesy of the University of Washington Photography Collection.*

First Up Mount Blackburn

By Dora Keen,
Photographs and
illustrations by
the author and
John E. Barrett,
except as
otherwise noted

Mount Blackburn (16,390 feet) rises in the central Wrangell Mountains. Lt. Henry Allen named the peak in 1885 for Joseph Blackburn (1838-1918), a U.S. Representative and U.S. Senator from Kentucky.

• C. M. MOLENAAR

No one had ever tried Mount Blackburn until

my expedition of the previous year. Mount Blackburn was only 16,140 feet high [16,390 feet by current surveys], only as high as the base of the great peaks of the Himalayas. It was just a little higher than Mount Blanc, and about as steep as the Italian side of the monarch of the Alps. Had it been in the same latitude I could have climbed it, as I had Mount Blanc, in two days, but the previous August four men and I, with three dogs, had spent thirteen days in the attempt and in the end had been obliged to give it up because our supplies had been calculated for a twelve-day ascent only.

My kindly, courageous, and efficient leader of the year before and the rest were scattered and unable to go, all but Mr. John E. Barrett, who had driven the dog team. He was to lead this year and to engage the other men, so he and I were the only ones, of our party of eight, who had ever been near the mountain before. On March 25, 1912, I had wired to him in Alaska that if conditions were favorable I should arrive at Kennecott, the starting point, at the end of the Copper River Railway, and four miles above the end of Kennicott Glacier,

on April 16th. He had merely replied, "Favorable. Come as quickly as possible." All preparations I had to work out alone, at once, and far away, and the previous expedition was the only one on which I had ever been. That I was only five feet tall would matter very little. Success would depend rather upon judgment, endurance, courage, and organization.

Thus was every condition reversed this time. It was winter instead of summer. I knew in advance the seriousness of the undertaking and this time there was no one to help me to organize the expedition.

I was going again because I had need of courage and inspiration and because on the high mountains I find them as no where else.

Success and safety would depend upon haste, and yet I could not reach Cordova before April 16th. Bad news greeted me. The season was a month early. One slide had already interrupted travel on the railroad for a week. The ice in the Copper River was breaking up. It might carve away the railroad bridge at Chitina any day. I had brought a German from Cordova, Mr. G.W. Handy, to be one of the expedition. He had been recommended as a good man and a good climber and had prospected near another side of Mount

Blackburn. The other six men were Axel Waldstrom, Bob Isaacson, "Bill" Lang, C.W. Kolb, John Bloomquist, and Mr. Barrett, all prospectors and all living within view of Mount Blackburn at the foot of Kennicott Glacier, up which lay the "easiest" way to our mountain.

At 5 o'clock in the morning on the 22nd of April we were off. Our 2,000 pounds of outfit had been hauled up the 200-foot wall of Kennicott Glacier by a pulley and stood lashed to the eight sleds and trailers to which the dogs were harnessed. It was only 18°, yet in an hour, just as the going became smooth, the snow began to soften. Spring had come. As we made camp on an "island" in the glacier that afternoon, for the sake of having timber, we were all exhausted and to come four miles had taken eleven hours of hard labor. The very next morning the best pulling dog of our nine escaped and went home.

To make speed we tried relaying the loads. One day we would put half ahead and the next day move camp still farther ahead with the other half, bringing up the first half at night. Still, by the third day it was clear that we had come too late to have an easy or quick approach to our glacier-surrounded mountain.

With temperatures around 18°, every morning about 1 o'clock in unheated tents the men would draw on their frozen shoepacks — I slept on mine to prevent their freezing — cook and eat breakfast and pack up while it was still dark and cold, in order to be ready to travel as soon as we could see, at 3:30. When it was cloudy we could not tell a hole from a hill nor even see the leader's snowshoe trail ten feet away. Mr. Barrett kept ahead with his "crevice puncher." Roping was unnecessary. Every day snowshoes had to be put on as soon as the sun shone, but even so by about 10 o'clock the cutting through of sled runners and dogs' feet would oblige us to stop for the day. All we could do then was to eat, sleep, wait for the night to give a crust and for the dawn to show the way.

At night the thermometer would drop to 12°, zero, or even 6° below, but by day it showed 59° or 70°, and in the sun even 96°. By day the glare made sleep difficult and we had hardly got to sleep after supper before we must get up again. On the third day, at only 3,300 feet, we had to resort to the oil stoves and they consumed as much time as oil.

Thus slowly in six days we raised nearly a ton of outfit 3,500 feet in thirty-one miles. Travel and spirits improved with elevation and the last day we made fifteen miles in seven and a half hours. Yet it was the 26th of April when we reached the foot of Mount Blackburn.

We had reached the main sources of Kennicott Glacier. In a horseshoe curve above us rose a majestic amphitheatre of lofty snow peaks, jagged ridges, and precipitous walls. Between the ridges tumbled the mighty ice falls of seven great glaciers. We seemed like atoms before these impregnable fortresses as we prepared to pit our human littleness against the pitiless forces of Nature. The snowy dome of Mount Blackburn lay nearly 11,000 feet above us.

We had noted the summer before that the flow of the avalanches from these steep glaciers at times extended three miles, so a mound in the center, out of the lines of flow and far from all walls, seemed the safest place for our base camp. Here dogs and sleds must be left with one man, Kolb, because of the crevasses and ice falls above.

Once at the foot of the mountain, we were all agreed that, although Barrett Glacier was the steepest of all, it offered probably the only route by which there was any hope of

On April 26, 1912 the Keen party arrived at base camp, at 5,500 feet, the last point at which dogs could be used to haul supplies. Mr. Kolb, one of the party members, stayed with the dogs.

ascending this side of Mount Blackburn at this time. I had named it for Mr. Barrett the year before.

Already at 11 o'clock the next morning our route and our success seemed determined, for starting at daybreak with fairly good snow, four men and I had reached 8,700 feet and were back before the slides had begun. There, in a snow dug-out to which supplies were now relayed, the three best climbers, Barrett, Handy, and Waldstrom would sleep the next night, after exploring the 3,500 feet above.

Again neither snowshoes nor creepers were required as another dawn found all of us leaving the base with more packs to start up the mountain. A half hour brought us to the first steep slope, and after an hour's steady snow ascent it was no longer possible to avoid the crevasses. From here up progress was slow as we threaded our way through a maze of crevasses to camp in their midst.

Even the miseries of a heavy pack were repaid by the sights about us, and once established on another mound at "Crevice Camp" — there could be no other name for it — there was nothing to mar the exhilaration of the scene. As the sun had grown hot, immediately on all sides the ice cliffs had begun to

112

break off and the powdery snow to slide from the walls of rock between which we were rising. We were safe from all slides and could enjoy their beauty to the full. In the Alps one keeps to the rocks and avoids glacier travel wherever he can, but at the same altitudes in Alaska all the rocks have a perpetual crest of ice hundreds of feet in thickness. When the thawing begins fragments fall; hence in Alaska the rocks are places to keep away from. If glaciers and snow ridges offer no safe route, the mountain cannot be climbed.

The slides were a subject of constant study; we could calculate how to avoid them and had time to observe their movements before venturing in their path, and the men assured me that "you could most generally always side-step them in time after you heard the first crack overhead." They had dodged them before now while hunting and prospecting.

"We've found a route up," said Mr. Barrett, as we set up our tents with our three explorers at Crevice Camp; but the gulch up which he pointed was so steep, so studded with bulging ice masses which must sweep us away if they broke off, and so near some rocks whence the ice was always breaking, that I hesitated.

"It's all right if we go early," he assured me. "But I tell you," and his face grew serious, "we'll have to go light and rush it; for that gulch is going to slide sometime, and if we keep a-traveling up and down it till we get all the stuff up, somebody's going to get killed. Just take food and what you have to have, and we men can sleep in the sun."

Thus were my carefully laid plans to be altered, almost daily, according to the conditions and the humor of the men — men, who think women whimsical.

Certainly our night among the crevasses emphasized the need for getting up and down the mountain as soon as possible; for fearful splits in the ice, apparently right under our tents, kept waking us, making us wonder whether we were about to be engulfed as we slept.

As the dawn showed the way amid the crevasses, we shouldered our packs. . . . It was the 30th of April. Fortune favored. The snow stayed firm and we rose rapidly merely with creepers and axes, no step-chopping, no roping, although for fully 3,000 feet the average angle of the slope was 60°. Twice the level showed 76°. Each took his own gait, the men's a top speed with rests, mine the slow but steady plodding of the Alps. My pack of 25 pounds exhausted me and, unasked, Isaacson and Lang generously added it to their already heavy loads. When there was ice underneath we went carefully. Crevasses were few and visible. The snow showed no tendency to slide. Our chief concern was due to the fearful ice masses which stood out to right and left, always one just overhead in our zigzag trail. Impressive as were their sizes and shapes, it was an anxious three hours and a half until we got above instead of below one after another that looked ready to fall on us. No icicles were breaking, no snowballs coming down, and yet we dared not relax our speed until at length we stood at the top of that perilous gulch. We had fixed 9 o'clock in the morning as the end of safe travel, and it was only eight. We had climbed about 3,500 feet in four hours and a half with all that was necessary to life for three days on our backs.

For the next hour we had but one thought — water — and no way to melt it except to hold tin cups full of snow patiently over candles. Just above and quite too near for safety, a sheer wall of ice 150 feet high seemed to block every path. To camp here seemed unsafe, to find a way up apparently impossible. On every side loomed huge blocks, pillars, and towers, as large as houses.

The only way led right under and between lofty ice needles fantastic in shape. As we clambered carefully around the snow-hidden holes between the shattered remnants of those that now lay prostrate, stopping when we dared, through spaces a few feet wide we could look down a sheer 6,500 feet to our base camp, and on far across Kennicott Glacier up to the very summits of Mount Regal and distant Mount Natazhat.

In Cordova Mr. Handy had had a small anchor made for throwing a rope over crevasses. By means of it a rope and then a man were quickly up the wall, at a point where the ice lay piled to within twenty feet of the top, without the delay of chopping steps, and soon all of us and our packs were safe.

We had reached 12,400 feet, and could now trace a route right up to the top. Indeed, the way seemed so clear that I estimated five to seven hours as all that would be needed to climb the 4,000 feet that remained, but it was impossible to proceed at once, for the snow had softened. It would be better to wait until daybreak.

The panorama was one to linger over, but a chill breeze decided us to dig "igloos" or caves in the snow. The shovel flew and soon I "holed in" to mine, which reminded me of a sleeping-car berth — if only it had been as warm. "The smaller the warmer," they said, but it had the chill of the grave, and I had had to leave blanket and sleeping-suit at Crevice Camp. Whenever I sat up or moved or arranged my hair, elbows and hair got full of snow. A flag pole marked each cave, lest someone step through the roof. The thermometer went down to 12° and even with mitts and sweater on in my fur sleeping-bag my feet were barely warm enough for me to sleep.

It was broad daylight when I awoke, to realize that I had not been called. Had the men then frozen to death? I wondered, as I hurried out to see. A snowstorm was raging. Stamping and tramping to keep warm, sitting on a snowshoe, or huddled over two candles trying to melt water and to warm it for tea or bouillon, I found five silent, cold, weary men. Unless we descended at once the trail would be covered and the rations for the summit depleted; but to venture down that fearful gulch in a blinding storm seemed to me out of the question. Moreover, I hoped that the weather would clear in time for us to go to the top and back without the added labor and danger of climbing down and up that gulch anew.

So we stayed, stayed three days, until the food was so nearly gone that there was no choice but to go down. Each day the storm had grown worse. Two feet of snow fell in 24 hours. By day I would lend my sleeping bag to two men at a time, who would take turns lying on it for two hours at a time, but to cover them I had only the maps of the now invisible glaciers. I had already lent both my extra sweaters. A snowshoe for a carpet kept our feet off the snow. I sat on my leather mitts, kept my hands in my arm-pits, and stamped my feet like the rest. At least numbers and candles made their cave warmer than mine. The next morning they dug me out three times and finally dug a small burrow off their cave for me. Outside it was warmer, but wet. They told me stories of their life in the wilderness, and always their talk was of timber and water and game.

On the 3rd of May we went out into a howling, freezing, driving snowstorm to grope

Tilting towers of ice (at about 12,200 feet) overhang the route to Blackburn's summit.

our way down the awful 3,500 feet that lay between us and more food.

"It don't look good to me," said my leader, as finally we found the top of the gulch. Without a word Mr. Handy took the lead, tested the snow, and started down. The slope was so steep and the snow so deep as to keep us wet to the waist half the time. Over crevasses and on down a now trailless path of danger, we seemed always to be just on the brink of some precipice or crevasse. We could not see fifty feet ahead, sometimes not twenty.

On went Mr. Handy, through all the hours never hesitating ... never afraid, merely shouting back occasional warnings of crevasses or of steep ice underneath. For the latter Lang would anchor his ax and "snub us down," [belay] and the rope stood every test. It was as cool and brilliant a piece of leadership as I have ever seen. In four hours we were safe down that gulch to Crevice Camp.

The next morning it was still snowing. Mr. Barrett wanted to go for wood, the Finn and the two Swedes for good, and they left us, here at 8,700 feet, on the 4th of May.

"To wait for the haymaker" — as Lang called the sun — to dry the bedding was the only way. Moreover, they thought that even when the storm ceased we should have to wait a week for that gulch either to slide or settle. Meantime the food would probably run short and the mountain grow too dangerous because of the rapidly advancing season. Mr. Handy said, "Don't turn back unless you want to. We will get up without them." I had brought food and fuel for five weeks.

Amid the yawning crevasses of Barrett Glacier, Mr. Handy, Lang, and I were all that were now left of the eight that had set out two weeks before for the summit of Mount Blackburn. We were only at 8,700 feet and it was already the 5th of May, but we were snow-bound, and "May and June are the months of slides" had been my warning before I started.

Mr. Barrett had wished to see how Kolb and the dogs were faring and had gone down to the base camp the day before with the three men that were homeward bound. Today he was to come up again, bringing his tiny wood stove and the wood from the hardtack boxes. Mr. Handy and Lang went down to meet him. With Kolb and the dogs to help, Mr. Barrett was bringing up a big load of supplies on a sled as far as the crevasses.

We seemed safe on our mound, safely away from all walls and far from all lines of breakage and flow. Suddenly a thundering roar made Lang step out. On the other side of the glacier, somewhere near our gulch, a great mass of ice had broken off and was falling. It had dropped 2,000 feet and came rolling onward like a great wave of surf and spray. It was flowing into the wide basin below us with a momentum which nothing could withstand. It was a mile away and on the side of the glacier where lay our trail to the base, and we were watching to see whether it would extend so far — when all of a sudden an icy, snow-laden gust told us to run for our lives to our dugout and, before we could get in, Lang and I were covered. We had got only a smart sprinkling, but the cloud of "spray" remained about five minutes or more.

We had all been thinking: what if a big slide were to come from our side of the glacier, from above us? It could not fail to sweep us away, tents and all. Mr. Barrett decided to go down to the base camp. The rest of us preferred to stay and to make overselves slideproof in a snow cave. By tunneling into the steepest slope of our mound we would be safe, no matter how many slides went down over us, provided only that our roof were solid. Hence the cave must be small, just big enough for us to live in; and we three did live in it for nine days. It was about the size of a bathroom and half as high, 10 feet by 6, with 4 feet to stand in. Anything left out in the storm was lost in an hour, so everything had to be stowed away inside. In one end I managed to raise my tent just enough for me to crawl into at night and keep my possessions dry.

The thermometer often went down to 21° inside, but we could not have heat lest we weaken our snow roof or run out of fuel, so between meals we would crawl into our sleeping bags. The hardest thing was to keep dry, for every time we went out we were in snow to our knees at the least and got wet all over, and the only way to dry anything was to sleep on it. Sometimes it would snow three feet in a day or a night. And yet, during the nine days in that snow cave we slept more, ate more, laughed more, even washed more than all the rest of the time put together, and I think the thing I minded most about the entire expedition was that there were days when there was not enough water for me to brush my teeth.

One day Mr. Handy said, "I think Barrett and Kolb will be wanting to turn back also; but I have spoken to Lang and he agrees that we two can get you to the top of the mountain alone, so don't you turn back, unless you want to."

On the 10th of May, the tenth day of the storm (which had abated a little), for the first time it seemed safe to descend far enough to meet Mr. Barrett and Kolb. Mr. Barrett was anxious lest his wife worry. Both wished to go back; and with them would go the remaining dogs. Thus did we burn our bridges behind us; but Mr. Barrett was to return in two weeks to search for us if we had not then appeared. We

Miss Keen crosses a crevasse during a snowstorm. Storms delayed the party and forced them to climb late in the season when avalanches and weak-crusted snow made their attempt even more hazardous.

turned and faced the wind to go back to our cave. The storm grew wild and we could barely follow our trail of two hours before.

For another three days the snow continued. We could do nothing but talk. Lang loved to repeat the German fairy stories of his childhood, "Snow White and Rose Red," and the rest, interlarding his philosophy of life. He was as simple as a child, although he was an old hunter and trapper from Eastern Ontario. The wilds had no terrors for him. . . .

Mr. Handy was the son of a German army officer. He was adventurous and daring by nature, but a disciplined soldier and always the first to subordinate his own interests to the good of the whole. He had been trained in a German technical school, had done his military service in Southwest Africa, and had mined in South America, Mexico, California, and Alaska. He had even been a cowboy in Texas.

On the 13th of May, there came a lull in the storm, and at last we could venture to the base camp for some necessaries. As we were upward bound, the skies cleared. The thirteen-day snowstorm was over. Although it was 9:30 at night the sunset was only beginning to fade as we got to our cave at Crevice Camp, and five hours later it was sunrise again as for the second time we were preparing to start up the mountain.

At dawn on the 15th of May, for the second time we lost sight of Crevice Camp, once again to strain every nerve to get up that gulch before the slides should begin. Once more we had left tents and stove behind, but this time I had insisted that the men take their bedding. So there were five loads for two men, there was no relay party, and the deep new snow would be certain to double the time; and the hours of safe travel had dwindled to the brief period of a dusk and dawn that could hardly be told apart. Indeed, all the conditions were changed, and the ascent would now be twice as hard as before the storm. The difficulties were as great or greater than the previous August when we had given up this route as too dangerous, but I knew my men and I trusted their judgment and ability.

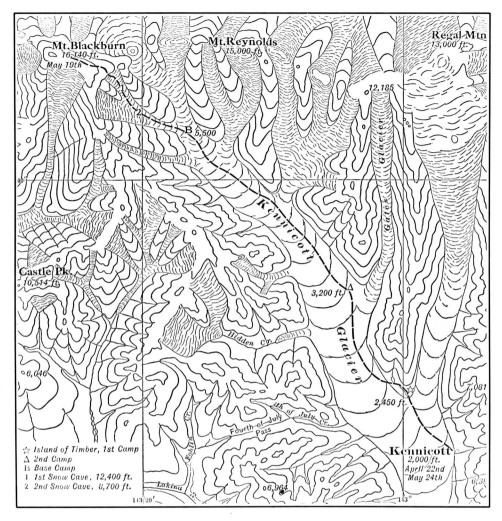

This map shows the route of the Keen party up Mount Blackburn, and the location of camps and snow caves where the climbers took shelter during their 33-day effort. Darker areas indicate glaciers.

The night was clear and I could drink in the beauty of it all while the men rested from their heavy packs. Lang would roll his pack off, exclaiming, "There, you've been lying on me long enough! It's my turn to lie on you awhile."

At 2 o'clock in the morning we were under the treacherous rock-cliffs and amid huge snowballs, tell-tales of slides. Lang pointed to the overhanging upper lip of a big crevasse beside us now drifted half full of snow, saying, "There, that's the kind of a place to get in if a slide comes." Hardly had he spoken when there was a loud report overhead as of an explosion, and we looked up to see ice cliffs descending upon us. "Come here!" cried Lang from behind, and as we were roped we had to, although the quickest way to safety lay ahead. As I turned, the tails of my snowshoes caught and I upset. Two of us had yet to cross a narrow slanting ledge of ice overhanging a crevasse, but somehow we reached shelter just in time to be half way under as the slide came on. As we crouched, "Dig in your ice pick!" were the last words I heard. A moment and it had passed, and for a second time we had only two inches of snow all over us, for an intervening gulley had most of the slide. The route the men had chosen *was* a safe one.

Once at the foot of the gulch, despite the softness of the snow the angle necessitated creepers. The sun was already hot as at 3:15 we began the ascent of that 3,000-foot nightmare gulch. To climb the first 150 feet I had to take hold of the rope, for it was 76° and all ice underneath, but Mr. Handy had not even chopped steps as he had taken the rope up to anchor it. The steeper the slope the better he liked it. He did not call the zigzag method climbing. He was never afraid, yet he never led us into danger. Until 9 o'clock we would be safe even here, and by that hour surely we hoped to be in our cave above the wall. A deep groove like a toboggan slide told where something had come down, and I was glad when the last pack and the last man were above instead of beside it.

Hauling seemed the quickest and easiest way for two men to get five packs up so steep a gulch. To a "sleigh" or "buggy," as he called it, made from two snowshoes, Lang would tie two packs at a time, and around an anchored ice ax Mr. Handy would "line them" up eighty feet at a time. I helped to haul or broke trail ahead. I had to choose the steepest places in order that the sled might slide; yet, work as we would, by 5 o'clock in the morning it would no longer slide either up or down. Trail breaking had become such deep, steep work that I was pressing first one knee and then the other ahead and still rising only three inches at a time. By 7 o'clock the snow was so soft and the slope so steep that bits of snow, "snowballs," were rolling down on us — warning of slides to follow. We were exhausting ourselves and still we were making no progress. It was time to be out of such a place, and yet we could not hope to get up the remaining 1,200 feet to our cave before the slides should begin. We were only two thirds of the way up the gulch, and I could not see even a safe place to camp. Indeed, to look up was appalling, for to right and left ice cliffs loomed threateningly overhead. It was the only time when I felt that we were really in grave danger and saw no way out of it; but Lang had more experience than I. "Why," he said, "we can camp most anywhere as far as that goes," and he pointed to the "shelter" of one ice mound after another as a good camp site! Under an eyelid of ice, as it were, deep in the recesses of a snow-filled ice cave, we spread our bedding and awaited the night. A great crack right across our roof warned us away from its edge. A fringe of icicles, like eyelashes, dripped merrily — so long as the sun was on them — giving us water.

We were safe from anything that might come, and yet I could not sleep for the thunder of the many slides on every side. None came near us until midday, when twice the deep rolling of falling ice made me sit up with a start just as a great mass went sweeping by. They were the most awe-inspiring sight that I have ever seen, so wonderful, so thrilling to watch, that I wished I did not need sleep. They passed so close that it was as if the American Falls at Niagara were suddenly overwhelming us. It was the most exciting day of the entire ascent. l nothing came over us, and at 3:30 in the afternoon I got up. The higher we rose the fewer the slides — but on the descent the opposite would be true. I looked down and there at the foot of our gulch, 2,000 feet below, lay the fragments of a great slide spread out like a fan. It had gone down since we had come up just there a few hours before. It was the third big slide we had escaped.

We had reached 11,000 feet, and still there was no crust as again we started upward at 10 o'clock in the evening, none until the cold breeze of dawn found us on a glazed slope where a crust left no foothold. Just as we seemed to have reached the top of the gulch bad crevasses caused delay. It grew late and we looked upward anxiously. Weary from lack of food we had to stop to eat in none too safe a place. At the top steps had to be chopped and when at length we were up, utterly weary from the disheartening struggle in kneedeep snow, the most we could do was to crawl into a shaded shelter as far as possible from the great ice wall above. For lack of a relay party and because of the advance in the season, it had taken thirteen hours to get merely food, bedding and essential outfit up 1,000 feet.

In the seventeen days since we had dug our first cave above this wall all had changed. New blocks had parted from it. The great 60-foot ice needles under which we had once hurried had fallen. Landmarks were gone and just to find the way up 200 feet again to our "igloo" and to dig it out took all that night. Only by the bare tip of a bamboo pole did we discover it. We had been four days regaining the 3,500 feet which we had before climbed in as many hours. For the second time we had reached 12,400 feet. Between 10,000 and 12,500 feet what appeared to be a volcanic ash discolored the snow.

At 9:30 in the evening it seemed as if we should really reach the summit that night. The slope was easier, slides were improbable so high up, and although snowshoes were still required, moccasins had replaced rubber shoepacks lest our feet freeze. We had only 4,000 feet to go, and to avoid further relaying the men decided to leave their bedding.

At midnight the wind pierced us as we exchanged snowshoes for creepers, only to need the snowshoes again when they were far behind. For an hour we were wallowing to our knees. Then a thin crust made us take to all fours, and still we broke through. For the breakfast halt we sought shelter but found none, until Lang dug a third cave. The distance had been considerable and although it was 3 o'clock in the morning we had reached only 14,000 feet.

An ocean of billowy clouds covered Kennicott Glacier. The earth lay hidden from view and only the mountain tops appeared as the tints of the dawn added the last touch to the most superb view of my life. As we watched, the peaks took fire and in a moment over the snow spires of Mount Reynolds the sun crept forth.

Although at 3:30 the thermometer showed only 6°, before we could start again trail breaking had become so arduous that it seemed best to wait for the shadows. With makeshift coverings and moving as the sun moved we slept a little. At 5 o'clock in the evening Lang started up the last 2,000 feet. He was ploughing to his knees and the slope had become steep enough for him to zigzag.

At 15,000 feet our packs made us begin to feel the altitude a little. Because of the moccasins my creepers refused to stay firm, and to rebind them was a long, cold process. We were not getting up very fast, but it was no place for a slip. At 9 o'clock at night we saw Lang depositing my bedding above, at the only level spot. Presently we also would be there with the shovel to dig a last cave, the fourth — for a brief rest. The next moment he was running down, pausing as he passed only long enough to say that he felt a little sick, and, since he "had no bet on getting to the top," he thought he would go down to his bedding and wait. After twenty-seven days of misery he had turned down within 500 feet of the top. Of the seven men in our party that had started, one alone remained.

It was zero at midnight. Even at sunrise it was only 3°. To thaw a tin of salmon over two candles took an hour. The final slope was steep and slippery, and even so high there were holes. We were a full hour climbing it, and when at length we thought the summit attained, we found that it was a half mile plateau on which a half hour's wandering and use of the level were necessary in order to determine the highest point. Indeed, at first a twin summit at least two miles away to the northwest appeared the higher one. [Modern

U.S. Geological Survey maps show the northwest point to be higher.] A long snow saddle connected them. Finally, however, at the northeast edge of the southeast summit we seemed to be standing on the top of Mount Blackburn, all that were left of us, two of eight. It was 8:30 in the morning and the 19th of May. Even a temperature of 6° and an icy gale from which there was no shelter failed to mar the satisfaction of achievement in the accomplishment of a difficult task. It had taken four weeks.

There was nothing to impair a view upon which our eyes were the first that had ever looked and the panorama seemed limited only by the haze of distance as we gazed a full 200 miles on every side.

With aching hands and in wind-hardened snow — for lack of any rock at all — we planted and guyed the bamboo flag pole which we had dragged up, burying beneath it a brief record of the first ascent of this great 16,140-foot subarctic peak.

After four hours and a half, relief from the cold wind became imperative and we turned downward to rejoin Lang below.

With crevasses opening all but under us as we waited for snow bridges to harden, three days of anxious work brought us to the base, and two days more to Kennicott on the 24th of May.

Because of the latitude, to climb up and down 11,000 feet of snow and ice had required 26 days. After 33 days entirely on snow and ice, of which 22 nights had been spent without tents and 10 days without fuel, we were back — back to wood and water, to green grass and spring flowers, to civilization and friends.

On Mount Blackburn and Mount McKinley, the discoverer of the North Pole has said, the problem of Alaskan mountaineering has been

Dora Keen uses an ice ax to dig a snow cave.

solved. The Parker-Browne expeditions and mine have proved that the secret of success lies in going early and using dogs. Our 1911 expedition had been the first to use dogs on a mountain and the one here recounted was the first to succeed without Swiss guides, the first to live in snow caves, the first to make a prolonged night ascent, the first to succeed on an avalanche-swept southeast side, and the only Alaskan ascent in which a woman has taken part — to the credit of the men be it said. We succeeded because one man cared to succeed.   ••

Sport hunting drew the largest number of recreational users to the Wrangells prior to 1979 when much of the region became a national monument. Many of these hunters were non-Alaskans and required the services of a guide. About 50 guides worked the Wrangell, Chugach, and Saint Elias area, some guiding only part-time, and horses made the work of packing supplies much easier.
• STEVE McCUTCHEON

A Mountain Playground

Sport Hunting

September 19. Cold, hungry, miserable in the swirling fog, Pete Serafin dedicated all his remaining endurance to staying high where he thought Dall rams ought to be. He followed the high ridges until 2 p.m. Finally the ridge dropped away to a huge basin, where the two rams Pete had spotted the day before were alternately feeding and watching by turns.

Pete studied the rams and the intervening terrain for an hour or more, estimating the approximately 600-yard range over and over in 100-yard increments. He reviewed the technological and trajectorial details, memorized on a hundred rifle ranges.

Pete licked his lips, nervously. Another night was near, there was no possibility of stalking to a shorter range. He was already a hard day's trek from his packboard. Time was running out.

The man licked his lips again, and again he measured the range with one eye squinted shut. Slowly, he bedded the rifle in his crushed felt hat on the shale.

Pete cranked the variable Leupold to 7-power and set the cross hair at one and a half body heights above the biggest ram's backbone. Softly, carefully — ever so gently — he squeezed the trigger.

Suddenly the big ram rolled out of his bed and flailed out of sight into the jumbled boulders far below. One shot.

— Dan M. Gish, "Lone Hunter
In The Wrangells," *Selected Alaska
Hunting & Fishing Tales, Volume Four*
(Anchorage: Alaska Northwest Publishing
Company, 1976), p. 32.

Hunting scenes such as this have been repeated countless times in the Wrangells. Sport hunting was the major recreational activity in the Alaska portion of the Wrangell-Saint Elias complex through 1978. Establishment of the national monument closed these lands to sport hunting, but under the newly-created park and preserve status, sport hunting is allowed in the preserve but not the park. In Kluane National Park, hunting has been prohibited since Kluane Game Sanctuary was formed in 1943.

Harvest of Dall sheep, the major game trophy in the Wrangells, is limited to animals with at least a seven-eighth curl on their horns. This translates to males generally older than six years. During the gold rush and mining periods, sheep were heavily hunted by subsistence and market hunters. Throughout the early 20th century, their numbers were greatly reduced on more accessible ranges.

The Wrangells have figured prominently in total Alaska sheep harvest. Through 1978, close to 30% of all sheep taken in the state came from here. Although the number of rams with a horn length in excess of 40 inches has been declining in recent years, Boone and Crockett Club records show that 68 of the top 200 listings were taken in the Wrangells, particularly near Chitina and Barnard glaciers. This area has been judged to contain the best habitat for production of trophy sheep in the state.

The number and quality of sheep has in turn attracted national and international hunters. Fifty percent of sheep hunters are not resident Alaskans, and under state law these hunters require services of a guide. An extensive guiding industry has developed in the Wrangell, Saint Elias and Chugach mountains with more than 50 guides working the area, at

Two successful hunters display their skins and horns from Dall sheep outside Tom Spersted's cabin in the Wrangells.
• BARRY SANTANA

least part-time, and most concentrating on sheep.

Compared to Dall sheep, all other big game species are but lightly used for sport purposes. Fly-in hunters stalk caribou from the Mentasta herd near Mount Sanford and Nabesna Road. The Chisana caribou herd, which ranges mostly outside the park and preserve boundary, has received increased hunting pressure the past few years.

Moose hunting has generally been limited to road corridors in the Wrangells and because of low populations, harvests have been small. Also because of reduced populations, hunting for this species has been prohibited along Nabesna Road in recent years. Several moose are taken each year on the Malaspina Glacier forelands. This small population is particularly significant because moose hunting in the Yakutat area has been closed for several years because of low populations.

Black and brown/grizzly bears are both sought by sport hunters, the latter often in connection with other species on a guided hunt. Near Malaspina Glacier guided hunts specifically for brown bears do occur. Near Yakutat hunters seek glacier bears, a blue-gray color phase of the black bear.

Sport Fishing

National park and preserve designation has no effect on sport fishing in the Wrangells, and fishing remains a significant recreational pursuit. Stream fishing on Alaska lands in the region is minimal because most streams are heavily silt laden and fast flowing in summer and greatly reduced in flow in winter. Within the Wrangell-Saint Elias complex in Alaska, only the Beaver Creek system north of White River; Hanagita and Tebay rivers south of the Chitina valley; and rivers in the Yakutat Forelands have clear water streams. Those near Yakutat nourish major salmon runs; those farther north support grayling (Beaver Creek) and rainbow trout (Hanagita and Tebay). Too, a small steelhead run comes up the Hanagita. Fishing in both Hanagita and Tebay rivers is considered excellent but because of difficult access, is only lightly pursued.

Major recreational river fishing centers around red salmon, and to a lesser degree,

Top • *Excellent trout, grayling, and ling cod fishing entice this angler to try his luck at Tanada Lake on the northern flanks of the Wrangells.*
• GERALD WRIGHT, NATIONAL PARK SERVICE

Left • *Alaska Natives use fish wheels to catch salmon on the Copper River.*
• JOHN & MARGARET IBBOTSON

king salmon runs on the Copper River. These red salmon, which spawn in clear lakes and outlet streams in the Wrangells and in the Gulkana River system, form a mainstay of the salmon fishery at Cordova. They are an important food resource for residents along the Copper River from Chitina to Chistochina. Here Natives catch salmon with a fish wheel, and by obtaining a subsistence fishing license, others may harvest them using a dip net. This technique involves standing in cold, murky, swift-flowing water holding a long-handled net and waiting for salmon to swim into it. Dip-netting takes place between Chitina and O'Brien Creek on the Copper River, and is an important recreational outlet as well as supplemental food source for many interior Alaskans.

Conflicts have developed in recent years of low salmon runs over allocation of fish between recreational and subsistence users near Chitina, and commercial interests on the lower Copper. New regulations affecting the length of the dip-net season and allowing for temporary closure at times of low escapement were put into effect in 1979 and were highly unpopular with recreational users.

Most recreational fishing in the interior Wrangells occurs on lakes. Tanada, Copper, Ptarmigan, and Rock lakes provide excellent lake trout, grayling, and ling cod. Summer access to these lakes is usually by floatplane although Tanada Lake can be reached by all-terrain vehicles from Nabesna Road. Both Tanada and Copper lakes are easily reached by snow machine in winter and are used for ice fishing. Scattered recreational fish camps on Tanada, and one each on Copper, Ptarmigan and Rock lakes offer varying levels of comfort and accommodation. Lakes in Chitina valley and Hanagita and Tebay river drainages contain rainbow, grayling, and other species, and are reached by floatplane. Both Tebay and Hanagita lakes have fish camps.

Several smaller lakes along both Nabesna and Chitina-McCarthy roads, Jack Lake, Long Lake, and Strelna Lake contain grayling and trout. Because of road access, these lakes receive substantial pressure from fishermen.

Kluane National Park offers fishing at a few points accessible by road as well as in the back country. A national park license is required.

A fisherman swings a heavy dip net into the Copper River near Chitina.
• SAM TAYLOR

Dust flies as hikers descend a slope into the Slims River valley in Kluane National Park. The park offers magnificent opportunities for outdoor enthusiasts but all overnight hikers must register with the park warden before leaving and upon returning from a hike.
• COURTESY OF PARKS CANADA

Backpacking

The region draws numerous hikers and backpackers. Easy access encourages most backpackers to explore either in the Chitina valley or off Nabesna Road where Jacksina Creek drainage is a preferred route. In the Chitina valley, backpacking centers around McCarthy. An interesting route follows the old mining road up Kuskulana River from Strelna, a relatively easy route to Kuskulana Glacier and magnificent views of Mount Blackburn.

Traveling up Nugget Creek from the trail's end provides good access to alpine areas and many square miles of hiking splendor.

One of the most intriguing, but difficult, hikes is along the historic Goat Trail up Chitistone Canyon to Skolai Pass. Initial access must be by plane, and can be expensive. Most people hike down the canyon (there is a small super-cub airstrip at upper Skolai Lake), and terminate at Glacier Creek, site of a good dirt airstrip.

Lack of major glacial rivers, less brush and a generally drier climate make the north side of the Wrangells, from Chisana to Horsfeld and south along Ptarmigan Creek, especially attractive to hikers. Access is by air to Chisana or the strip at Horsfeld. Floatplanes can also be landed at Ptarmigan and Braye lakes.

Mountain Climbing

Mountainous terrain of the region provides virtually all types of climbing experience. Opportunities range from glacier and ice-filled climbs of Mount Sanford and Nabesna Glacier; to rigorous, high-altitude mountaineering on the Icefield Ranges near Mount Saint Elias and Mount Logan; to steep, rock-walled climbs in Chitistone Canyon. In 1979, estimates determined that non-Alaskan climbers spent more than 3,000 visitor days in the Wrangells. Many were Japanese climbers. Local climbing clubs in Anchorage and Fairbanks sponsored numerous climbing events. Within Wrangell-Saint Elias National Park and Preserve, current National Park Service policy is to allow traditional access and support of climbing expeditions, such as aircraft landings on glaciers, to continue.

Water Activities

Water-based recreational use other than for fishing is limited. Rafting on the Copper River from Chitina to the delta has been growing steadily in popularity over the last decade. The Chitina River also offers good rafting, but so far rafters have not taken advantage of this route. Alsek and Tatsenshinni rivers far to the south attract increasing numbers of kayakers and rafters.

Winter Recreation

At present little winter recreation occurs in the Wrangell-Saint Elias region. The Wrangells, particularly the mid-Chitina valley, have high cross country skiing potential because broad river flats which hinder overland travel in summer become natural routes of travel for skiers in winter. ••

Upper left • *Climbers tackle the 12,010-foot summit of Mount Drum in the western Wrangells. In 1979 non-Alaskan climbers spent an estimated 3,000 visitor days in the Wrangells.*
• THIRD EYE PHOTOGRAPHY

Lower left • *Dan Metz climbs a ridge leading to Nikolai Butte (6,000 feet), 16 miles southeast of McCarthy in the Wrangell Mountains.*
• JIM VICKERY

Left • *Nick Olmsted shows his best skiing style in this high-speed telemark down a slope near Chitistone Pass. Camille Rodrigues watches from about 5,600 feet on the slope.*
• BILL GLUDE

People and the Economy

The small community of McCarthy lies at the end of a 63-mile extension of the Edgerton Highway from Chitina. It serves as a jumping-off point for those exploring the southern Wrangells.
• GERALD WRIGHT

McCarthy and tiny Chisana represent the

only permanent communities remaining in the Wrangells. Haines Junction, population about 500, and Yakutat, population about 450, are the largest commercial centers in the Saint Elias area. Outside these enclaves, some individuals live on homesteads, alone or in small groups scattered throughout the region. In the Wrangells most of these groups are clustered along the Chitina-McCarthy and Nabesna roads, and in the Dan Creek-May Creek area. Guiding, trapping, and prospecting provide some income for many of these residents. A few near Strelna farm marginal agricultural land. Others work outside the region in seasonal jobs, and still others have no discernable means of income. The very few people living in remote areas of the Saint Elias range follow a subsistence lifestyle. All these people have one trait in common, a high degree of independence and a desire to be free of government restraint.

Residents of communities along the state highway system surrounding the area — Chitina, Copper Center, Glennallen, and Gakona for example — use the Wrangell and Saint Elias mountains on a transient or seasonal basis for guiding, mining, subsistence, and recreation, primarily hunting.

Glennallen, center of the regional highway system, provides services such as high school education, banking, food, clothing, and medical care. Most other communities along the highways are marked by a roadhouse, school and a few homes.

Native and non-Native residents of a particular community generally occupy different areas. Non-Native residents tend to be very independent, for the most part conservative, and opposed to any form of government control.

Natives of the interior Wrangells belong to the Ahtna culture and seem to be less homogeneous in their attitudes and values than the non-Native community. Many Natives, particularly the elderly and those in the smallest villages, have retained patterns of living from decades past.

Younger people in the villages were confronted by the economic bonanza of the trans-Alaska pipeline and more recently each village has had to face the complex task of making land selections under terms of the Alaska

Opposite, left •
The trans-Alaska pipeline dips into a low area near Squirrel Creek, at about mile 80 of the pipeline corridor which runs from Valdez on Prince William Sound to Prudhoe Bay on the arctic coast. Mount Wrangell (14,153 feet) rises in the distance with Mount Zanetti (13,000 feet) to the left.
• GEORGE HERBEN

Below • *Tom Bell, an Athabascan from Lower Tonsina area, has lived most of his life around Chitina and is one of the last remaining residents of the Native village there. Tom told the photographer about drinking the sweet sap of tree bark once his mother had prepared it a certain way. "We ate roots. We dug them up. Wasn't anything else. They were pretty good eating," says Tom.*
• MATTHEW DONOHOE

Above • *Chitina has no central plumbing and drinking water must be hauled from the local creek. Julie Baugnet, an itinerant artist who answered an ad the town placed in a journal, pulls the sled on which the water jugs are resting. In return for room and board and little salary, Julie has stayed on as the town's artist.*
• MATTHEW DONOHOE

Right • *Neil Finnesand, 97, stokes a stove he has had for 40 years. "A fellow from McCarthy, Bill Berry, made it. He could make almost anything," says the old-timer. Neil, born in Norway in 1883, came to Alaska in 1904 and has not been Outside since. He participated in the White River gold rush in 1913: "They say 5,000 people went in there but quite a few people turned back. Took out about $1 million in gold. The news came out in the middle of summer. It was a stampede. People came from all over; Fairbanks, Valdez, Cordova. Everybody wanted to get rich."*
• MATTHEW DONOHOE

Left • *Duffy's Roadhouse near the end of Nabesna Road lures (from left) Maggie Joe, Bill Joe and Jack John of Chistochina in for coffee. Roadhouses like Duffy's, once absolutely necessary, were spaced about a day's travel apart along the road. Even today the roadhouses are important gathering places.*
• MATTHEW DONOHOE

Native Claims Settlement Act. A small number of Native residents are active in Ahtna Regional Corporation set up under the act and have experienced a marked change in lifestyle. Tasks of corporate management, negotiations with other businesses and Native corporations, and planning and implementing the terms of the act are new experiences for these individuals.

Most residents of the Copper River valley rely on a mix of temporary, often seasonal, employment opportunities and quasi-subsistence activities. Employment is most often with state education and government agencies, utility companies, and supply services along the highway. However, traditional regional living and economic patterns are changing, primarily because construction of the trans-Alaska pipeline thoroughly modified the economy, injecting massive amounts of money into the area and creating many jobs. By some estimates, more than 60% of the men in the region worked on jobs that were related to the pipeline.

Abrupt termination of pipeline activity, combined with what has been a continual decline in recreational travel on the Alaska Highway and Tok Cutoff, has severely affected the local economy. (Increasing use of self-contained vehicles by travelers has further depressed the roadhouse-lodging industry.) Unemployment is high. Hopes for sustaining the economy and services generated by the pipeline have now largely been dashed. On the other hand, there is a reticence, and probably an inability, to return to the pre-pipeline economic base and activities.

The region lacks a good economic foundation and, beset as it is by land selection uncertainties, the future, while potentially bright, remains clouded. ••

Clockwise from above

• Bob Buck, principal of Nabesna Road School, plays kick ball with his entire student body.

• Jeweler Art Koeninger works at his trade in a building he owns, the oldest building in Chitina.

• Arleen Dummler plays with her puppies near Strelna along the McCarthy road. Arleen's family owns 160 acres in the area.

• Guide Lee Hancock's horses graze among hoarfrost-covered grass and trees.
• ALL PHOTOS BY
  MATTHEW DONOHOE

Land Status in the Wrangell-Saint Elias Area of Alaska

Jumbled mounds of rock signify the terminal moraine of Kennicott Glacier. On the horizon (left) rises Mount Blackburn. The contact zone between different geological formations on Donoho Peak (6,696 feet) is visible at right center, and Root Glacier and Stairway Icefall are at far right.

• GEORGE HERBEN

*Children enjoy a
summer cruise
on Jack Lake on the
northern flanks of
the Wrangells.
Tanada Peak
(9,240 feet) rises in
the background.*
• GEORGE HERBEN

Since Alaska Native Claims Settlement Act

Editor's note: The
future of Wrangell-
Saint Elias was an
important issue for
many Alaskans and
Outsiders for years.
Study after study
sought to determine
the most appropriate
use of these lands.
Finally Congress, in
November 1980, passed
a bill creating the
Wrangell-Saint Elias
National Park and
Preserve. The
information in this
chapter relating to the
park question was
prepared well before
passage of this bill, and
is included as
background on factors
influencing the
final bill.

was passed, lands of possible national significance were the object of intensive study by the National Park Service; and to a lesser degree by U.S. Forest Service, Heritage Conservation and Recreation Service, the state, and other groups. Opinions of future management of these lands were as numerous as the agencies and people who wished to use them.

The potential of the Wrangell-Saint Elias complex for national park status was long recognized and there was little objection to the ultimate establishment of a park; arguments instead have revolved around the size of the park. Conservationists supported more, and development-minded individuals supported less, land in park status. Until May 1980, proposals ranged from the 15.8-million-acre Wrangell-Saint Elias National Park proposed in early 1977 under a bill in the U.S. House of Representatives (HR 39) to the 1975 state of Alaska proposal for a Wrangell Mountains National Park of 3.7 million acres and a Wrangell Mountains Preserve of nearly 2 million acres. [Resolution of the issue in November 1980 created a national park and preserve of 12,318,000 acres.] The park was to be traditional with no sport or subsistence hunting and no mining, whereas hunting and

subsistence use were to be allowed in the preserve.

Also, the joint Federal-State Land-Use Planning Commission proposed a Wrangell-Saint Elias National Park of about nine million acres with traditional national park use. Lands near Tanada Lake and Jacksina Creek, those north of White River, and around McCarthy, Kennecott, and May Creek were not included within the proposed park but were to be placed under park service administration pending a final decision on the park boundary. Because of possible national importance of other resources, particularly minerals, these lands were to receive more detailed study before drawing the final park boundary.

Merits of these and other proposals were debated. In 1980 the U.S. Senate considered bills which would settle the lands issue. Bills similar to those debated by the Senate, but different from the 1977 version of HR 39, passed the House of Representatives in 1978 and 1979 under the name of HR 39. Under the 1979 bill, up to 12.3 million acres was to be set aside as national park, preserve, and recreation areas in the Wrangell-Saint Elias region in Alaska.

Delay in final lands solution proved unsettling to the region both economically and socially. Most residents seemingly were

resigned to a National Park Service presence in the area and to the likelihood of more restrictive land managment than had existed in the past. Some individuals even welcomed a park service presence.

Debate over Alaska lands settlement and resulting publicity has focused national attention on these lands and their recreational potential. Sport hunting, long the most important and at times almost the sole recreational use on these lands, was banned under monument status but reinstated in preserve areas under the new designation. Non-consumptive recreational use, particularly backpacking, has increased dramatically.

HR 39 offered a compromise in regard to sport hunting. Both the preserve and national recreation area designated in the bill, consisting of about four million acres, would have been open to sport hunting. These lands included most of the Chitina valley north of the river to Barnard Glacier, Jacksina Creek drainage and all lands north of White River, and Malaspina Glacier forelands. The preserve's boundaries were drawn primarily on the basis of Dall sheep harvest. Officials estimated that a substantial percentage of areas of past sport hunting would still be available as hunting territory under the preserve.

Another factor softening opposition to National Park Service administration in the area was the bleak economic picture. The promise of increasing tourism, with resulting employment opportunities, was one of few potential bright spots on the horizon. Recreational visitation for 1979 was estimated at 18,000 visitor days.

Even with settlement of the park issue, a large question remains as to the potential uses and ultimate disposition of Native selections

within the region. Ahtna Corporation is entitled to about 705,000 acres, primarily in township-sized parcels which fall in the lower Chitina valley, on the western forelands of the Wrangells, and along Nabesna Road. Some of the lands have high recreational potential, Strelna and Tanada Lake for example, or are very scenic.

Chugach Regional Corporation has

Tom Spersted, longtime resident and registered guide, checks out his cabin at May Creek in the Wrangells.
• BARRY SANTANA

Below • *Nabesna, near the end of Nabesna Road, has a population of less than 25. The tiny settlement was known as Khiltat after Indians of the area. When mining developed here early this century, the town became known as Nabesna.*
• STEVE McCUTCHEON

Right • *"Everybody just calls me Ray," says the attendant as he pumps his non-electric gas pump in Chitina. Ray has the cheapest gas in the area, cheaper even than the big stations in Glennallen.*
• MATTHEW DONOHOE

Right • *The Wrangells are prime Dall sheep habitat as this trophy room at Devil's Mountain Lodge shows.*
• GEORGE HERBEN

Left • *Harley King tries his carpentry skills at Long Lake, between Chitina and McCarthy, while his dog keeps watch.*
• GEORGE HERBEN

selected, because it was prevented from choosing lands elsewhere, several thousand acres in the Bremner River drainage and also at Icy Bay. Because the corporation does not consider the Bremner River acreage to be equal to its traditional use areas, the organization is seeking a legislative solution to trade them for other more appropriate coastal lands.

In the Wrangells, large blocks of privately owned land that can be subdivided, developed, and sold are surrounded by national park and preserve. Impact of development of these private inholdings remains a great unknown and is a source of concern for individuals who support management by ecosystem units and for inholders.

More than 50,000 acres of state land in the Chitina valley near McCarthy is being considered for subdivision and sale to private individuals under the state land disposal program. Several thousand acres of privately owned land at McCarthy, Kennecott and Nabesna have recently been subdivided into approximately five-acre lots. Private subdivisions in general have not taken into account sewage disposal and water problems. Roads that have been built often erode quickly, becoming impassable. Problems such as access and diminishing timber supplies suitable for construction and heating have not been addressed.

Decisions on the future of the Wrangell-Saint Elias lands in Alaska are difficult. The choice between preservation and use is seldom black-and-white and compromises are helpful, but in the end, choices have to be made. This mountain wilderness is a special place, to be used and enjoyed, but in such a way that its qualities remain unimpaired.   ••

Aerial view of Kennicott Glacier (right), Gates Glacier and Packsaddle Island (left), University Range of the Saint Elias Mountains (left background), and Mount Saint Elias (pyramid-shape), and Mount Logan on the horizon.
• GEORGE HERBEN

RICKS COLLEGE
DAVID O. McKAY LIBRARY
...URG, IDAHO 83440

Alaska Geographic® Back Issues

The North Slope, Vol. 1, No. 1. Charter issue of *ALASKA GEOGRAPHIC®*. Out of print.

One Man's Wilderness, Vol. 1, No. 2. The story of a dream shared by many, fulfilled by few: a man goes into the bush, builds a cabin and shares his incredible wilderness experience. Color photos. 116 pages, $7.95

Admiralty . . . Island in Contention, Vol. 1, No. 3. An intimate and multifaceted view of Admiralty: its geological and historical past, its present-day geography, wildlife and sparse human population. Color photos. 78 pages, $5.00

Fisheries of the North Pacific: History, Species, Gear & Processes, Vol. 1, No. 4. Out of print.

The Alaska-Yukon Wild Flowers Guide, Vol. 2, No. 1. First Northland flower book with both large, color photos and detailed drawings of every species described. Features 160 species, common and scientific names and growing height. 112 pages, $10.95

Richard Harrington's Yukon, Vol. 2, No. 2. A collection of 277 stunning color photos by Canadian photographer-writer Richard Harrington captures the Yukon in all its seasons and moods, from Watson Lake to Herschel Island. 103 pages, $7.95

Prince William Sound, Vol. 2, No. 3. Out of print.

Yakutat: The Turbulent Crescent, Vol. 2, No. 4. Out of print.

Glacier Bay: Old Ice, New Land, Vol. 3, No. 1. The expansive wilderness of Southeastern Alaska's Glacier Bay National Monument unfolds in crisp text and color photographs. Records the flora and fauna of the area, its natural history, with hike and cruise information, plus a large-scale color map. 132 pages, $9.95

The Land: Eye of the Storm, Vol. 3, No. 2. Out of print.

Richard Harrington's Antarctic, Vol. 3, No. 3. The Canadian photojournalist guides readers through remote and little understood regions of the Antarctic and Subantarctic. More than 200 color photos and a large fold-out map. 104 pages, $8.95

The Silver Years of the Alaska Canned Salmon Industry: An Album of Historical Photos, Vol. 3, No. 4. Out of print.

Alaska's Volcanoes: Northern Link in the Ring of Fire, Vol. 4, No. 1. Scientific overview supplemented with eyewitness accounts of Alaska's historic volcano eruptions. Includes color and black-and-white photos and a schematic description of the effects of plate movement upon volcanic activity. 88 pages, $7.95

The Brooks Range: Environmental Watershed, Vol. 4, No. 2. Out of print.

Kodiak: Island of Change, Vol. 4, No. 3. Out of print.

Wilderness Proposals: Which Way for Alaska's Lands?, Vol. 4, No. 4. Out of print.

Cook Inlet Country, Vol. 5, No. 1. A visual tour of the region — its communities, big and small, and its countryside. Begins at the southern tip of the Kenai Peninsula, circles Turnagain Arm and Knik Arm for a close-up view of Anchorage, and visits the Matanuska and Susitna valleys and the wild, west side of the inlet. 230 color photos, separate map. 144 pages, $9.95

Southeast: Alaska's Panhandle, Vol. 5, No. 2. Exploring Southeastern Alaska's maze of fjords and islands, mossy forests and glacier-draped mountains — from Dixon Entrance to Icy Bay, including all of the state's fabled Inside Passage. Along the way are profiles of every town, together with a look at the region's history, economy, people, attractions and future. Includes large fold-out map and seven area maps. 192 pages, $12.95.

Bristol Bay Basin, Vol. 5, No. 3. Explores the land and the people of the region known to many as the commercial salmon-fishing capital of Alaska. Illustrated with contemporary color and historic black-and-white photos. Includes a large fold-out map of the region. 96 pages, $9.95.

Alaska Whales and Whaling, Vol. 5, No. 4. The wonders of whales in Alaska — their life cycles, travels and travails — are examined, with an authoritative history of commercial and subsistence whaling in the North. Includes a fold-out poster of 14 major whale species in Alaska in perspective, color photos and illustrations, with historical photos and line drawings. 144 pages, $9.95.

Yukon-Kuskokwim Delta, Vol. 6, No. 1. Out of print.

Aurora Borealis: The Amazing Northern Lights, Vol. 6, No. 2. The northern lights — in ancient times seen as a dreadful forecast of doom, in modern days an inspiration to countless poets. Here one of the world's leading experts — Dr. S.-I. Akasofu of the University of Alaska — explains in an easily understood manner, aided by many diagrams and spectacular color and black-and-white photos, what causes the aurora, how it works, how and why scientists are studying it today and its implications for our future. 96 pages, $7.95.

Alaska's Native People, Vol. 6, No. 3. In the largest edition to date — result of several years of research — the editors examine the varied worlds of the Inupiat Eskimo, Yup'ik Eskimo, Athabascan, Aleut, Tlingit, Haida and Tsimshian. Most photos are by Lael Morgan, *ALASKA®* magazine's roving editor, who since 1974 has been gathering impressions and images from virtually every Native village in Alaska. Included are sensitive, informative articles by Native writers, plus a large, four-color map detailing the Native villages and defining the language areas. 304 pages, $19.95.

The Stikine, Vol. 6, No 4. River route to three Canadian gold strikes in the 1800s, the Stikine is the largest and most navigable of several rivers that flow from northwestern Canada through Southeastern Alaska on their way to the sea. This edition explores 400 miles of Stikine wilderness, recounts the river's paddlewheel past and looks into the future, wondering if the Stikine will survive as one of the North's great free-flowing rivers. Illustrated with contemporary color photos and historic black-and-white; includes a large fold-out map. 96 pages, $9.95.

Alaska's Great Interior, Vol. 7, No. 1. Alaska's rich Interior country, west from the Alaska-Yukon Territory border and including the huge drainage between the Alaska Range and the Brooks Range, is covered thoroughly. Included are the region's people, communities, history, economy, wilderness areas and wildlife. Illustrated with contemporary color and black-and-white photos. Includes a large fold-out map. 128 pages, $9.95.

A Photographic Geography of Alaska, Vol. 7, No. 2. An overview of the entire state — a visual tour through the six regions of Alaska: Southeast, Southcentral/Gulf Coast, Alaska Peninsula and Aleutians, Bering Sea Coast, Arctic and Interior. Plus a handy appendix of valuable information — "Facts About Alaska." Approximately 160 color and black-and-white photos and 35 maps. 192 pages, $14.95.

The Aleutians, Vol. 7, No. 3. The fog-shrouded Aleutians are many things — home of the Aleut, a tremendous wildlife spectacle, a major World War II battleground and now the heart of a thriving new commercial fishing industry. Roving editor Lael Morgan contributes most of the text; also included are contemporary color and black-and-white photographs, and a large fold-out map. 224 pages, $14.95.

Klondike Lost: A Decade of Photographs by Kinsey & Kinsey, Vol. 7, No. 4. An album of rare photographs and all-new text about the lost Klondike boom town of Grand Forks, second in size only to Dawson during the gold rush. Introduction by noted historian Pierre Berton: 138 pages, area maps and more than 100 historical photos, most never before published. $12.95.

COMING ATTRACTION

Alaska's Mammals, Vol. 8, No. 2. Featuring approximately 80 of the mammal species that occur in Alaska — from the awesome brown/grizzly bear through the spectrum to the tiny creatures such as the deer mouse and the voles, and including the marine mammals. Beautiful color photos augment detailed text that includes descriptions of the mammals, their range and life history and their importance to man. To members May 1981. Price to be announced.

Your $20 membership in The Alaska Geographic Society includes 4 subsequent issues of *ALASKA GEOGRAPHIC®*, the Society's official quarterly. Please add $4 for non-U.S. membership.

Additional membership information available upon request. Single copies of the *ALASKA GEOGRAPHIC®* back issues available, per listing here. When ordering please add $1 postage/handling per copy. To order back issues send your check or money order and volumes desired to:

The Alaska Geographic Society

Box 4-EEE, Anchorage, AK 99509